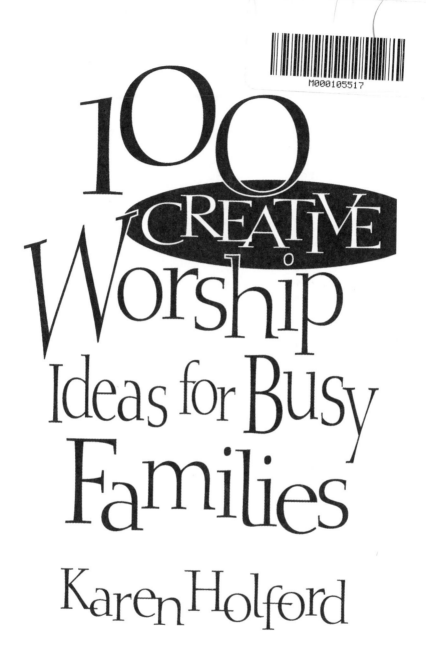

100 CREATIVE Worship Ideas for Busy Families

Karen Holford

Pacific Press®
Publishing Association

Nampa, Idaho | Oshawa, Ontario, Canada
www.pacificpress.com

Cover design by Steve Lanto
Inside design by Kristin Hansen-Mellish

Copyright © 2014 by Pacific Press® Publishing Association
Printed in the United States of America
All rights reserved.

Additional copies of this book may be obtained by calling toll-free 1-800-765-6955 or online at http://www.adventistbookcenter.com.

Library of Congress Cataloging-in-Publication Data
Holford, Karen.
    100 creative worship ideas for busy families : from the author of 100 Quick & easy creative activities for sabbath / Karen Holford.
        pages cm
    ISBN 13: 978-0-8163-5017-9 (pbk.)
    ISBN 10: 0-8163-5017-5 (pbk.)
    1. Families—Religious life. 2. Children—Religious life. I. Title. II. Title: One hundred creative worship ideas for busy families.
    BV4526.3.H635 2014
    249—dc23
                                2013038321

November 2013

Dedication

To you, wonderful parent,
who wants to share God and His love
with your lively, curious, and creative children,
even though your life is frantically busy,
because you know that this is the most important job
you'll ever do
in the whole wide universe.

May you be blessed, may your heart be encouraged,
and may your faith be strengthened,
as you pray, love, laugh, talk, create, discover,
strengthen faith, build character,
and grow closer to God and to each other.

Love the Lord your God with all your heart and with all your soul
and with all your strength.
These commandments that I give you today are to be on your hearts.
Impress them on your children.
Talk about them when you sit at home and
when you walk along the road, when you lie down and when you get up.
Deuteronomy 6:5–7, NIV.

Contents

Introduction

How to Help Your Children Grow Spiritually

The most important gift we can give our children is the desire to love God and to follow and serve Him.

- You can help by being a positive role model, because your children will be inspired and encouraged by your faith.
- Take the time to talk to your children about your own faith and relationship with God, in ways that they can understand.
- Pray for your family and your children, as well as for yourself. Let your children see and hear you praying for them. Share suitable stories of answered prayer with your children to help them develop trust in God.
- Help your children to look for answers to prayer but also to understand that God knows best, and sometimes the answers come in ways that we're not expecting, or even wanting.
- Experience God's grace and forgiveness for yourself so that you can pass this on to your children. Grace is about God's loving us no matter what we have done, just because we are His children. This is one of the most beautiful aspects of the Christian faith.
- Learn how to put God's grace into action in your family by offering forgiveness and showing acceptance when your children make mistakes or accidentally break or spoil something.
- Deal with your children in the way God has patiently dealt with you. Think about how God has gently disciplined you before you consider how to discipline your children in a way that will bring them closer to God.
- As you parent your children, aim to show them God's amazing love for them by the way you manage them with caring gentleness. Read 1 Corinthians 13 and think about how that kind of love can make a difference to your parenting.
- Encourage your children to develop their own spiritual relationship with God by spending a few minutes a day reading a Bible verse or book and praying.
- Help them to discover and use their own spiritual gifts and to look for God working in their lives.

Guidelines for Great Family Worships

Here are some guidelines to help your family have interesting and creative worships.

- Keep your family worships simple. You might like to use a children's devotional book or Bible study guides during the week, and make weekend worship times special.
- Plan ahead for worships, and gather the materials you need well before time.
- Invest in the best! Buy good books from your local Christian Book Store, seek out and rent good Christian DVDs, and buy interesting Bible games and activity books.
- Keep worship times free from discipline and criticism. Make them positive experiences: fun, interesting, brief, happy, and loving. This is what your children will remember the most.
- Use the worships to learn Bible stories, learn how to make good choices, follow God's guidance, develop a prayer relationship with God, learn about God's creation, memorize scriptures, experience the joy of serving others, learn worshipful songs,

and enjoy being Christians.

- Remember that children learn in different ways, and make sure that your worships contain practical illustrations, crafts, memorable stories, and physical activities.
- Use the everyday events that happen to you and your children to teach them about God. Opportunities for spiritual teaching are all around you once you start to look, and these are often the best ways to help your children learn about God. This book also includes lots of worships that can be blended into your usual family routines with very little effort.

Making a Worship Supply Box

It can be very helpful to create a worship box so that most of the things you'll need are all together and ready to use. Here are some things that may be useful to put in the box:

- A child's Bible
- This book, and other helpful worship books
- Safe scissors
- Adhesive tape
- Glue stick
- White paper
- Colored paper
- Colored cardstock
- Marker pens
- Permanent pens
- Clear acetate
- Pencils
- Eraser
- String
- Balloons
- Crayons
- Paper plates
- Stickers
- Brass fasteners
- Envelopes
- Bubbles
- Magazine pictures
- Bible storybooks
- Musical instruments
- A soft scarf for a blindfold
- Brown lunch sacks
- Fabric, felt, and craft scraps
- Interesting nature items and stones
- Small objects mentioned in Bible stories
- Colored buttons

Using the Worship Activities

- Every child and every family is different, so not every activity will suit every child or family. It is up to you to choose the activities that suit your family's needs.
- Activities that may not fit now may be more suitable in a year's time.
- Many of these worships are designed to need very little preparation, because parents are usually very busy. Save time by sending send your children to find the worship supplies while you read what to do with them.
- You may want to have a simple worship on weekdays, and save some of the more complex or longer worships for the weekends.
- All the worships ideas include other options in case they suit your family better or you don't have everything you need for the first worship idea. These other ideas can be developed to give you and your family even more worship activities.
- Some families like to repeat the worship activities that they enjoy, so make a note of the ones your family would like to try again.

Music for Worship

- Use tapes of children's worships songs to add music to your worship.

- Buy some videos of children's Christian songs for your children to watch and sing along with.
- Make or buy a collection of simple musical instruments that your children can play during worship.
- Create your own praise songs by using tunes you already know and adding your own words. Ask your children for ideas.
- Add actions to songs to help active children enjoy the music.

SECTION I

Worships About God

1

Create a Creature

Although humans can create many wonderful things, they can't create life. Only our amazing, creating God can design and shape living, breathing creatures.

Bible connection:

"God said, 'Let the land produce living creatures according to their kinds: the livestock, the creatures that move along the ground, and the wild animals' " (Genesis 1:24, NIV). See also Psalm 104. We may be able to make model animals, but only God can make creatures that live and move and breathe.

THINGS YOU NEED:

- A generous supply of newspapers, junk, string, crepe paper, tissue, wire coat-hangers, clean yogurt cartons, tubes and boxes, etc.
- Scissors
- Stapler
- Sticky tape, paper clips, etc.

Worship activities:

1. Read the Bible verse. Ask what it might have been like for God to create so many different creatures that live, move, and eat in so many different ways.
2. Work together as a family to create a model of a completely new kind of bird or animal using your craft supplies and junk.
3. The creature must be able to move in some way, such as flap its wings or bend its legs when you pull some strings.
4. Make sure that everyone is involved in designing and making the creature.
5. Stop after 15 minutes and see how well your creation works.
6. Discuss what you will call your creature, where it will live, and what it will eat.
7. Compare your creature to a real animal. How good is your creation compared to God's creation? Isn't God amazing to create so many different creatures so perfectly?
8. If you were God, which animal would you have enjoyed making the most?

Prayer:

- Choose your favorite animals or birds. Praise or thank God for at least three of their special features. Thank God for the way He has made each of you so wonderfully too.

Other ideas:

- Make your own individual creatures, instead of working as a group.
- Draw plans and designs for your animals instead of making them.
- If you are at the beach, in a park, or in a forest, try making your creatures out of the natural materials lying around on the ground.

2

Filled With Wonder

What are the wonderful things that inspire you to praise God for His creation? Is it a rainbow, how we breathe, a newborn baby, a mountain, the sea, a butterfly, a patch of bluebells, a whale?

Bible connection:

Psalm 8 or Psalm 19. We are surrounded by thousands of wonderful details of God's incredible creation. Being filled with wonder increases our faith in God.

THINGS YOU NEED:

- A collection of interesting natural objects, such as flowers, seeds, a piece of wood, animal skin, stones, shells, bones, etc.
- Pictures of amazing landscapes and scenery from the Internet, old calendars, books, etc.
- Pencils and paper (optional)

Worship activities:

1. Read the Bible verses and talk about any moments of wonder you have experienced recently. Children often have a natural sense of wonder and curiosity. Remind them of a time when they watched an ant, a bee, or another creature.
2. Let each person choose one of the natural objects or pictures you have collected.
3. Allow two minutes for everyone to explore their object carefully and to notice everything wonderful about it. They can write down these details if they wish.
4. Then let everyone introduce their item of wonder to the rest of the family, describing its special characteristics and talking about how perfectly it has been created.
5. Talk about what fills each of you with wonder. Is it something beautiful, tiny, huge, dramatic, mysterious, or unexpected?

Prayer:

- Write a psalm of praise together. Use the wonderful objects you have explored to inspire your praise-psalm prayer.

Other ideas:

- Collect rugs, hot drinks, pillows, binoculars or telescopes, flashlights, and books about stars. Find a dark place where you can lie down and watch the stars with your children. Identify planets and constellations. Talk about the wonders of the universe and God's amazing creative power.
- Go on a wonder-wander. Give everyone a bag in which to collect three natural things that fill them with wonder. Be careful not to take items that will damage the environment. Afterward, "show and tell" your discoveries, describing why they are so amazing, and what they teach you about God.

3

Rainbow Praise

Whenever we see rainbows, we're reminded of the story of Noah and God's promise to us. Rainbows can also remind us of the beautiful rainbow of glory shining around God's throne.

Bible connection:

"A rainbow that shone like an emerald encircled the throne" (Revelation 4:3, NIV). God's glory shines in a whole spectrum of colors. Make a rainbow that praises His glory and love.

THINGS YOU NEED:

- Large sheets of white paper, pencil, and eraser
- Marker pens in rainbow colors

Worship activities:

1. Talk about rainbows. When did you last see a rainbow? What do rainbows mean to you? What do you like most about rainbows? Etc.
2. Draw seven concentric arcs on the white paper to create the outline of a rainbow. Use a variety of colored pens to write a rainbow of praise on the paper. Do this as an individual or group project.
3. Use the colors and praise categories listed below:
   - Red—praise God for saving you and forgiving you
   - Orange—thank God for providing for you
   - Yellow—praise God for healing people or for keeping you healthy
   - Green—praise God for His creations
   - Blue—thank God for preparing a future in heaven for you
   - Purple—praise God for His love
   - Violet—write a verse from the Bible that praises God

Prayer:

- Read what you've written on your praise rainbows.
- Or make seven cards, colored according to the list above. Write each of the different praise categories on them and put them in a bag. Take turns drawing a card from the bag and praying a sentence prayer for the praise category that has been selected.

Other ideas:

- Use colored paper to make rainbow collages, bunting flags, or paper chains. Write praises on them according to the colors listed above.
- Staple sheets of different colored paper together to make a book of rainbow-colored pages. Let younger children write, draw, or stick pictures of some things they want to thank God for that are the same colors as the pages.
- Make a rainbow fruit platter together, arranging different-colored fruits in rows. Thank God for all the fruits. Praise God, using the categories listed above, as you eat through the delicious layers.

An Advertisement for God

Today we are surrounded by advertising for all kinds of things. Some of the advertisements are clever, interesting, or artistic. How would you design an attractive advertisement for God?

Bible connection:

"No one has ever seen God; but if we love one another, God lives in us and his love is made complete in us" (1 John 4:12, NIV). How can our lives be advertisements for God's love?

THINGS YOU NEED:

- Large sheets of paper as big as you can find
- Thick marker pens, tape, and scissors
- Pencils, erasers, and scrap paper for working out designs
- An assortment of magazines with examples of advertisements

Worship activities:

1. Read the Bible verse.
2. Give everyone a magazine and allow one minute for them to find their favorite advertisements.
3. Show the ads you have chosen and tell why you liked them.
4. Discuss how different ads appeal to different people. Look at how the colors, words, and pictures have been used to attract your attention.
5. Talk about how you could design an ad for God's love. Whom do you want to appeal to? What are their greatest needs? What would attract their attention?
6. Then ask each person to design an ad for God's love. They can cut pictures and words from magazines if they wish.
7. When everyone has finished, showcase your designs. Look at the different ways each of you have advertised God's love.
8. Then ask how you can be advertisements for Jesus. What can each of you do and say to be a living, walking, talking, smiling advertisement for God's love?

Prayer:

- Pray that you'll be good advertisements for God's love. Ask God to show you how to share His love with the people in your home, neighborhood, school, workplace, and community.
- Make a prayer poster, cutting words and pictures from magazines and arranging them in an attractive collage.

Other ideas:

- Older children might like to design an advertisement using a computer
- Christian T-shirt companies often have clever designs and thought-provoking slogans. Maybe you could turn one of your ads into a wearable T-shirt design?

5

Being Still With God

Our lives can be incredibly busy. Take time out to be quiet and to feel how refreshing it is to be still, to listen to God, to pray, and to think about His love.

Bible connection:
"Be still and know that I am God" (Psalm 46:10, NIV). When we stop and sit quietly for a while, God can have our full attention.

THINGS YOU NEED:
- A quiet corner or room with a soft rug and comfy pillows and chairs
- Soft, instrumental worship music and a CD player
- Safe candles, battery-operated lanterns, or Christmas lights
- Anything that will transform your room into a tranquil place

Worship activities:
1. Our lives are often very busy and noisy. It can be hard to find the time and space to be quiet and still for a while. But spending time being quiet with God, listening to His love and hopes for us, and thinking inspiring thoughts can be both comforting and energizing.
2. Make your peaceful space as inviting and lovely as possible.
3. Read the Bible verse and talk for a few moments about what it means to be still with God and to imagine He is right there in the room. Explain that you will do this just for a few moments, because being quiet and still can feel quite strange when you're not used to it.
4. Pray that God will make Himself known to each of you in the stillness.
5. Ask everyone to think about how much God loves them or to imagine that He is giving them a big hug or that they are sitting on His lap. Imagine what He most wants to say to each of you today.
6. Print out the children's version of "The Father's Love Letter" and give it to one of your children to read during the stillness. http://www.fathersloveletter.com/kids/.
7. After you have been quiet for a while, ask your children how it felt to be still and experience God. What did they think about? What did they learn about God or themselves? What new ideas did they have about God's love for them?

Prayer:
- Thank God for what each of you experienced in the stillness. Thank Him for the time and space to calm down and listen to Him. Thank Him for His loving care for each one of you.
- Or pray silent prayers for a short time, followed by a family hug.

Other ideas:
- Find an outdoor place to be quiet together: in a forest, by a lake, in a quiet corner of the park, in your yard, etc.
- Try having five to ten minutes of quiet time in your family as often as you can. Read one verse or a short Bible story, to focus your thoughts on God, before having some quiet time together.

Searching for God

As followers of God, we need to keep looking for Him, learning about Him, and discovering what He wants us to do for Him.

Bible connection:

"You will seek me and find me when you seek me with all your heart" (Jeremiah 29:13, NIV). Just like children playing hide-and-seek, God wants us to search for Him and He wants us to find Him. As we search for Him, we will discover more about Him, and we will come to love Him more.

THINGS YOU NEED:

- 10 envelopes
- Paper, marker pens, scissors, and one sheet of the paper cut into 10 slips
- A large red heart of cardstock or paper cut into 10 pieces, like a jigsaw puzzle
- Sheets of paper or cardstock, one of them as big as the heart
- Adhesive

Worship activities:

1. Prepare for worship by writing a Bible reference about God on each of the 10 slips of paper. Put one slip and one piece of heart jigsaw into each envelope. Hide the envelopes around your family worship room.
2. You might choose from these verses: Psalm 23:1; Psalm 139:7–12; Psalm 103:1–5; Psalm 103:8–12; Psalm 103:13–18; Psalm 145:3–5; Psalm 145:15, 16; Psalm 145:17–20; Isaiah 6:2, 3; Isaiah 30:18, etc. Or use your own favorite verses about God's love, kindness, forgiveness, glory, etc.
3. Read Jeremiah 29:13. Talk about what it means to seek God when we can't see Him. How do we search for God, and why do we need to search for God? What difference does searching for God make to our lives?
4. Then send your children on a search to find all the envelopes.
5. Open the envelopes together and help your children look up the verses and read them. Write what you learn about God from each of the verses on the separate jigsaw pieces.
6. Then make the jigsaw together, pasting the finished jigsaw onto a sheet of paper or cardstock to make a heart covered with descriptions of God.

Prayer:

- Draw two hearts, one inside the other, on sheets of cardstock or heavy paper, to make a heart-shaped frame. Draw a frame like this for each person. To avoid rips, cut out the frames after you've written on them.
- Write prayers between the lines of the heart frames, asking God to help you search for Him and find Him. Then cut out the frames. Look through the heart shapes as a reminder to search for God's love.

Another idea:

- Beside one of the envelopes, hide a gift, such as a small book, that will encourage your children to seek God in some way.

7

The Light of the World

Jesus is the Light of the world. He came into our dark world to light up God's character and to show us a safe pathway to heaven.

Bible connection:

"When Jesus spoke again to the people, He said, 'I am the light of the world. Whoever follows me will never walk in darkness, but will have the light of life' " (John 8:12, NIV).

THINGS YOU NEED:

- A collection of different kinds of lights, or make a list of the different lights around the home
- Paper, pencils, white adhesive labels, and pens
- A solar-powered object, or a candle and a hand mirror
- Tealight candles and a dish, or battery-operated tealights

Worship activities:

1. Read the Bible verse and talk about Jesus being the Light of the world. We often think of Jesus being a light in the darkness—but many kinds of lights can help us understand more about Jesus.
2. Look at the collection of lights you have found, or go on a light hunt around your house. Look for power lights, standby lights, warning lights, nightlights, table lights, candles, flashlights, security lights, emergency lights, etc.
3. Think about lights outside—car lights, street lights, traffic lights, lights on emergency vehicles, spotlights, illuminated signs, lighthouses, etc.
4. List the various lights you've found and what they can teach you about Jesus. He lights up our life. He shows us the way; keeps us safe; warns us; takes away our fear; helps us know when to stop, wait, and go; makes our lives beautiful; helps us to avoid dangers, etc.
5. Show how a solar-powered object works. Talk about how we can be solar-powered by letting Jesus' light shine on our lives or how we can be like mirrors behind candles, reflecting His light into a dark world.

Prayer:

- Give each person a tealight candle and a sticky label. Cut the labels so they will fit around the tea-lights.
- Ask each person to write on their labels how they would like to reflect God's love in the world. Stick the labels around the tea-lights.
- Place your tealights in a safe dish, light them, and pray together.

Other ideas:

- Give each person a sheet of tracing paper and a permanent marker pen. Cut the paper to wrap around a glass candle lantern or jar, with a small overlap for sticking the edges together.
- Write "Jesus is the Light of the world because . . ." and then write your ideas on the paper in an attractive way. Wrap the papers around the lanterns, stick the edges together, and light candles inside them.

8

God's Hats

God has lots of different jobs to do. But there's one He likes the best ...

Bible connection:

"See what great love the Father has lavished on us, that we should be called children of God! And that is what we are!" (I John 3:1, NIV). God loves being our Father.

THINGS YOU NEED:

- Lots of different hats, or pictures of hats, illustrating some of God's roles:
- A firefighter's hat—we can call on God in emergencies
- A policeman's hat—He keeps us safe and shows us the way to go
- An old-fashioned hat—God has always been there, and He never goes out of fashion
- A construction worker's helmet—God is preparing a place for us in heaven
- A judge's wig—God is the most merciful Judge ever!
- A Santa Claus hat—God is much, much better than Santa! He gives us good gifts, whether we deserve them or not, every day of the year!
- A foreign hat—God cares for everyone all over the world
- A crown—God is our King
- A crazy hat/headdress—some people think God is crazy—but He is the wisest person ever
- A hat that your children know as "Dad's hat"—hide this until you need it

Worship activities:

1. Show your children the different hats you've collected.
2. Talk about the different "hats" you wear as parents and the various responsibilities you have, besides being a mom or dad.
3. Look at each hat in turn and talk about God's work as a builder, a firefighter, a merciful judge, etc.
4. Now show the "Dad's hat." Ask your children how it reminds you of God's special work, the work He enjoys the most.
5. Read the Bible verse and think about what it means to be children of God. Talk about the special ways God has lavished His love on you in the past week.

Prayer:

- Pick up each hat in turn and thank God for doing the role that it represents.
- Pray the Lord's Prayer together. Make up actions to accompany the phrases, to add a fresh dimension to this familiar prayer.

Other ideas:

- Make a Father's Day card for God, thanking Him for lavishing His love on you.
- Ask your children to imagine they could spend a day with God as a loving Father. Invite them to draw pictures or write a schedule of how they would like to spend their time with Him.

9

God's Love Wreath

God is love, and His love has many wonderful dimensions. Make a wreath together to celebrate the different aspects of His love.

Bible connection:

1 Corinthians 13:4–8. This passage describes some of the many practical ways in which God loves us. Look up other verses about God's love too.

THINGS YOU NEED:

- 1 sheet of cardstock at least 12 inches (30 cm) square or cut cardboard from a large box
- Two plates of different diameters to help you draw a ring/wreath in which the band is at least 2 inches (5 cm) wide and the diameter of the outer circle is about 12 inches (30cm)
- Various colored papers, crepe paper, scrapbook paper, etc.
- Marker pens, scissors, and pencils
- Glue stick or double-sided tape
- Heart-shaped templates

Worship activities:

1. Use the two plates to draw two concentric circles on the cardstock. Cut out the center of the circle and around the edge of the widest circle so that you are left with a flat ring of cardstock. Cover the ring with attractive paper, or wrap strips of crepe paper around it. Cut neat heart shapes out of the colored paper scraps, varying the colors, sizes, and shapes of the hearts.
2. Read the Bible passage and make a list of all the ways God shows His love to us. Add other thoughts and ideas about God's love that aren't found in these verses.
3. Give each person a few paper hearts and ask them to write a Bible verse about God's love on their hearts or to write a description of God's love ("God's love is patient"), etc.
4. Roll just the edges of the hearts gently around a pencil so that they curl like petals, to add some dimension to the hearts.
5. Arrange the hearts around the wreath so that all the descriptions of God's love can be read. Fill any gaps on the wreath with small cut-out hearts or other attractive craft supplies.
6. Hang the heart-wreath where everyone can see it to remind them of God's wonderful love.

Prayer:

- Give each person a sheet of attractive paper or a blank greeting card. Invite them to write a love letter to God, as a prayer, and to thank God for all the wonderful ways in which He loves us.

Another idea:

- Make a heart wreath filled with Bible promises and give it to someone who needs encouraging or cheering up.

Our Invisible Friend

When Jesus left His friends on earth, He promised to send them the Holy Spirit, who could be with all of them, all the time, wherever they were.

Bible connection:

John 16:12–15. The Holy Spirit guides us, inspires us, comforts us, teaches us, and gives us special gifts.

THINGS YOU NEED:

- Drinking straws
- 2 or 3 cotton balls, balls of rolled up tissue, or ping pong balls for each person
- Various objects that illustrate the work of the Holy Spirit, labeled with Bible verses: a comforting blanket or hot-water bottle (Comforter—John 14:16); a picture of a dove (Peace-Bringer—Matthew 3:16,17); a compass, remote-controlled toy, or GPS system (Guide—John 16:3); gift bag (Gift-Giver—1 Corinthians 12:1–11); tool box or apron (Helper—John 14:16, 17, 26); batteries or electric extension cable (Power source—Acts 1:8)
- A few large, strong balloons
- Permanent marker pens

Worship activities:

1. Place all the balls on a smooth, shiny floor. Give everyone a straw. See how quickly your family can use the straws to blow the cotton balls from one end of the room to the other.
2. Talk about how hard it is to control the balls, even when you're trying to blow them in a straight line. How is your breath like the Holy Spirit? He is trying to guide us, but it's not always easy, because we often wander off in random directions.
3. When Jesus was on Earth, He could only be in one place at a time. When He left Earth, He sent the Holy Spirit so that He could be everywhere.
4. The Holy Spirit has lots of special jobs. Give each person an object and a Bible verse to look up. Then share what you've learned about the Holy Spirit's work from the Bible verses and the objects.
5. How is the Holy Spirit working in the lives of your family members? Tell each other about the times when you have seen the Holy Spirit at work in their lives.

Prayer:

- Give a flat balloon to each person. Our lives are like flat balloons until we're filled with the Holy Spirit. Blow up the balloons. How are they different from the flat balloons? Using permanent markers, write prayers on the inflated balloons. Ask the Holy Spirit to fill you and transform your lives.

Another idea:

- Send your children on a treasure hunt around your home using your cell phones (mobile phones). Give your children a phone and talk to them, or message them, guiding them to a treasure or to you. Discuss the importance of listening carefully to the Holy Spirit's instructions.

Worships That Lead Your Children to Jesus

HOW TO LEAD YOUR CHILDREN TO JESUS

GOD LOVES EVERYBODY

GOD'S LOVING RULES KEEP US SAFE

BROKEN RULES HURT US

EVERYONE HAS BROKEN GOD'S RULES

GOD WANTS TO SAVE US!

JESUS DIED TO SAVE US BECAUSE HE LOVES US

JESUS DIED SO WE DON'T HAVE TO!

WE CAN CHOOSE TO FOLLOW JESUS

JESUS MAKES US NEW

JESUS HELPS US GROW MORE LIKE HIM

How to Lead Your Children to Jesus

"Jesus said, 'Let the little children come to me, and do not hinder them, for the kingdom of heaven belongs to such as these' " (Matthew 19:14, NIV).

The importance of winning children

Recent research has helped us to understand that 70 to 90 percent of adult Christians first accepted Jesus as their Savior before the age of 13. So, it's up to 10 times easier to lead a child to Christ than an adult. This means that one of the most important jobs in the world is helping children make their decision to follow Christ. See http://www.barnaresearch.org.

Our responsibility as parents is to work hand-in-hand with the Holy Spirit to make sure that nothing in our power is stopping the children from coming to Jesus and accepting His gift of salvation. Then, once they have accepted Jesus, we need to continue working with the Holy Spirit to affirm their decision and nurture their simple trust into a strong and mature faith.

We mustn't be afraid of inviting children to accept Jesus, just because we think they can't understand everything or because we feel they're too young to be baptized. God is always delighted when children choose to follow Jesus!

When is a child ready to accept Jesus?

It's important to pray for the children in your sphere of influence. Be open to the Holy Spirit's guidance when you are looking for the best time to invite them to follow Him. There are some very simple signs that a child may be ready to accept Jesus as his or her Savior. The child:

- knows that God loves him or her in a very special way,
- loves Jesus and longs to learn about Him and follow Him,
- prays to God and looks for answers,
- chooses to do the right thing even when it is hard,
- understands when he or she has done something wrong and needs to ask God's forgiveness,
- wants to help others and be kind to them.

A child's steps to Jesus

When you feel prompted by the Holy Spirit, use these main steps for leading a child to accept Jesus as his or her personal Savior. Each step is supported with Bible verses, with ideas to help you personalize your faith story, and with ways you can help your child to understand and apply the steps to his or her life.

1. God loves everybody (1 John 4:8; Jeremiah 31:3)
2. I know that God loves me because . . . (Tell your children how you know God loves you.) How do you know God loves you? (Help your children to find some evidence that God loves them.)
3. Because God loves us, He has given us some good rules so we don't hurt Him or each other (Exodus 20:1–17). We call them the Ten Commandments.
4. Can you help me make a list of some of these good rules? (Work with your

children to make a list of commandments.) Shall we check if we're right and find out what the rest of the good rules are?

5. When we break these good rules, it's called sin; and sin hurts God, other people, and ourselves (1 John 3:4).

6. Last week I sinned by (tell your children about a simple and specific way that you sinned), and it hurt God, me, and someone else. Can you think of a time when you did something wrong and it hurt you or someone else? (Wait for your children to respond.) Did you know that God was hurt too?

7. Everyone has broken some of these rules and is a sinner (Romans 3:23). Sadly, when we sin, we have to die forever. That's quite a scary thought—

8. But God loves us, and He doesn't want us to die forever! So He sent Jesus to die in our place, instead of us (John 3:16).

9. Isn't that amazing? I'm so glad that Jesus has died in my place because (share one of your reasons). Jesus would have come and died if you or I were the only person in the world who had ever broken God's good rules. That's because He loves us so much!

10. When Jesus died in our place, He had never sinned. So God brought Him back to life to save us (1 Corinthians 15:3, 4).

11. Now we don't have to die forever. One day we can live in heaven with God instead! That's the best gift I can ever imagine. What do you think about what Jesus has done for you?

12. So when we believe in Jesus and accept that He died in *our* place for *our* sins, *we* are *completely* forgiven (1 John 2:1, 2). We just have to pray "I am so sorry, God, for hurting You by breaking Your good rules. Please forgive me because Jesus has already died for me. Amen."

13. Each of us has to make our own choice to accept Jesus' death for our sins and to become His children (John 1:12). Would you like to accept Jesus as your Savior today?

14. When you invite Jesus into your life, He'll help you to become like a new person! You won't *want* to do any more wrong things because you love Jesus and Jesus loves you (John 3:3–7; 2 Corinthians 5:17). But we still go on making mistakes, and God will always be ready to forgive us again.

15. Jesus wants to help you become more like Him. Once you've accepted Jesus, you can grow more like Him by exploring the Bible, praying, worshiping Him, and helping other people (Luke 2:52). What would you like to do to make sure you keep learning about Jesus?

Sample child's prayer for accepting Jesus:

Dear Father God,

Thank You for loving me so much! I love You too!

I am sorry that I have broken Your good rules and sinned.

And I am sorry that my mistakes have hurt You and hurt me and hurt other people too.

I want to accept Jesus as my Savior, because I believe He died to save me from my sins.

Thank You for loving me so much that You made a way for me to be forgiven.

Thank You that I can now live with You forever.

Please help me to obey Your good rules and always follow Your plans for my life.

In Jesus' Name, Amen.

⬤

God Loves Everybody

God loves everyone equally, no matter what they have done or who they are. He made each person, and He loves each of us as if we're the only person in the world.

Bible connection:

"This is love: not that we loved God, but that he loved us and sent his Son as an atoning sacrifice for our sins" (1 John 4:10, NIV). God loves everyone so much that He sent Jesus to die for every person, whether they love Him or not.

THINGS YOU NEED:

- Pictures from magazines with photos of people from around the world
- Photos of each person in your home
- Paper, paper glue, scissors, marker pens, and superstrong glue
- A large red heart cut from cardstock, along with leftover cardstock scraps
- Hole punch
- Thread, yarn, or twine

Worship activities:

1. Write the Bible verse on the large heart. Punch some holes along the lower sides of the heart so you can hang pictures from them.
2. Paste the photos of your family onto paper or leftover cardstock and cut them out. Leave a small tab above each person's photo. Punch a hole in each tab and hang the photos from the heart.
3. Find pictures of people from all over the world, so that you have a wide variety. Paste them to leftover cardstock, cut them out, leaving tabs above each photo. Punch holes in the tabs, and hang them from the heart too.
4. Talk about everyone in the world being tied to God's heart because He loves them all the same, regardless of what they look like, where they live, what they do, and whether or not they love Him.
5. Tell your children that God always loves them—even when they make mistakes or forget about Him or disobey Him. Nothing can separate them from God's love. Read Romans 8:38, 39.
6. Cut two small identical cardstock hearts. Write Romans 8:38, 39 on one heart and your child's name on the other heart. Stick them together with strong glue to illustrate that God will never, ever stop loving them.

Prayer:

- Hold hands and thank God that nothing can ever separate you from His love. Or make a card to thank Him for His incredible love.

Another idea:

- Cut several strips of paper dolls, holding hands, and fasten them together in a long row to make a garland. Help your children write "God will always love you!" on each doll.

12

God's Loving Rules Keep Us Safe

Sometimes we can find rules frustrating because they seem to restrict our freedom, or they make us feel guilty if we break them. But rules are an important part of keeping everyone safe. God gave us His rules because He loves us and wants everyone to feel safe, loved, and happy.

Bible connection:

"Keep his decrees and commands, which I am giving you today, so that it may go well with you and your children after you and that you may live long in the land the LORD your God gives you for all time" (Deuteronomy 4:40, NIV).

THINGS YOU NEED:

- Paper, pencils, scissors, and marker pens
- Small heart-shaped box (optional)
- Red paper cut into five hearts that will fit easily inside the box if you have one

Worship activities:

1. Read the Bible verse and John 14:15. Ask why keeping God's commands shows that we love Him.
2. Make a list of some of the important rules in your home, school, and community. Which rules help you to love other people? Which rules help you to love God? Which rules help you to love and take care of yourself? Discuss why these rules are so important.
3. What would happen if everyone ignored the rules? Would your home, school, or community be a happy place to live if everyone broke the rules?
4. Read the Ten Commandments in Exodus 20. Cut the five hearts in half and write a summary of each commandment on a separate half, so they can be placed, in turn, into the heart-shaped box.
5. Pick up each commandment as you put it into the box, or onto a pile, and discuss how it helps us to love God and to love each other.
6. Then read Matthew 22:37–39 and write a summary of the verses on the lid of the box. You can cover the lid with red paper if you wish.
7. All of God's commandments are His gifts of love, to help us and protect us.

Prayer:

- Thank God for giving us His important rules to keep us safe. Let each person choose one of the Ten Commandments and thank God for the ways in which it keeps us safe from harm.

Another idea:

- Play one of your family's favorite games together, such as a simple Bible game. As a parent, openly disobey the rules, by turning over more cards than you should, etc. See how your children respond to your rule breaking. Then talk about why rules are important and how God's rules are much more important than the rules of a game.

13

Broken Rules Hurt Us

When we break God's rules, we hurt, God hurts, and other people hurt.

Bible connection:

"These are the commands, decrees and laws the Lord your God directed me to teach you . . . so that you, your children and their children after them may fear the Lord your God as long as you live by keeping all his decrees and commands that I give you, and so that you may enjoy long life" (Deuteronomy 6:1, 2, NIV). God promises that keeping His commandments will help us to have happier lives.

THINGS YOU NEED:

- Appropriate newspapers—one per person, or several pages each
- Marker pens, paper, pens, and scissors

Worship activities:

1. Read Deuteronomy 6:1, 2.
2. Give each person a newspaper. Ask them to find all the stories of people who have caused hurt and sadness by disregarding God's loving rules with actions such as stealing, killing, hurting, lying, etc.
3. Cut out all the stories, and then sort them into piles according to which commandment they have broken. Circle any descriptions of the pain and distress that these people have caused others. Think about what might have been different if they had obeyed God's commandments.
4. Alternatively, choose a Bible family. Look at the commandments the Bible characters broke, and see how this hurt the various people in their families (e.g., Jacob and Esau's families; Abraham; David, etc.).
5. Remember that God loves each person, and He doesn't want anyone to be hurt. Look at each hurt person through God's loving eyes. How does He feel about their hurt? How does He feel about the wrongdoers? (Remember that He loves them just as much as He loves the people they hurt.)
6. Thank God for loving us, whether we have broken His commandments and hurt other people or we have been hurt by other people.

Prayer:

- Pray for those who were hurt by the rule breakers you found in the newspapers.
- Ask God if there is something you and your family can do to show them His love and care in their painful situations.

Another idea:

- Give each person a white heart cut from quality paper. Ask them to write their name on it. This represents a totally sinless life. Cut a larger white heart to represent God. Explain that lots of people can be hurt when one person sins, and lots of people can be sad when one person is hurt because of sin. Stack your hearts on top of God's heart. Take turns putting your name on top of the stack and ripping through all the layers of hearts. This shows how breaking God's rules causes pain and damage.

14

Everyone Has Broken God's Rules

Every single person, except Jesus, has broken God's rules. We are all hurting, and we all hurt other people and God.

Bible connection:

"All have sinned and fall short of the glory of God" (Romans 3:23, NIV). God is glorious beyond anything we can imagine. Compared to Him, we are so broken and tiny.

THINGS YOU NEED:

- The longest measuring tape you can find
- Paper and coloring materials

Worship activities:

1. Read the Bible verse. Discuss your ideas about what God is like. Read Revelation 4 for a description of His glory. He is glorious beyond anything we can imagine or understand.
2. Invite someone to draw a quick picture of the scene in Revelation 4, using lots of colors, or to write "God's Glory" in large colorful letters.
3. Take out your measuring tape and have fun measuring your different heights and the lengths of your fingers and feet, etc.
4. Then explain that if we wanted to measure God's glory with the tape, it would have to be longer than the distance from the earth to the sun. But we have only this small tape for now. So let's imagine that the length of this tape represents God's glory.
5. Stretch out the tape along the floor. Lay the picture or words of God's glory at the very end of the tape, near the highest numbers.
6. Then have everyone look at the very first and smallest measure on the tape. What can you think of that is as small as this tiny measure? An ant, a crumb, etc.
7. Explain that because we have all sinned and broken God's rules, we are a long way from God's glory and the way He first created us to be. We are the size of the very tiniest measure compared to God. But He loves us just as we are. He sent Jesus to fill the huge gap between the two ends of the tape so that we could be close to Him again.

Prayer:

- Kneel next to the "God's Glory" end of the measure. Imagine God in all His glory and praise and worship Him.
- Then kneel at the other end of the tape and thank God for loving you, even when you sin; make mistakes; and hurt Him, others, and yourself.

Another idea:

- Find an artist's impression of God's glory. Print it in color or look at it on the Internet. Or you may find a picture in a Christian magazine or Bible study guide. Look at how glorious it is, and then invite each person to draw the tiniest speck possible with a black pen, to represent themselves and to illustrate how very different we are from the magnificence of God.

15

God Wants to Save Us!

Jesus chose the most amazing way to show God's love for us so that we could never be in any doubt about His love.

Bible connection:

"This is how we know what love is: Jesus Christ laid down his life for us" (I John 3:16, NIV). When we think about what Jesus did for us, we understand more about His amazing love and more about loving each other.

THINGS YOU NEED:

- Cross shape cut from cardstock or an old box
- Lots of red hearts cut from paper
- Marker pens
- Paper adhesive
- Bible concordance or Internet search engine

Worship activities:

1. Read I John 3:16.
2. Give everyone a few red paper hearts and ask them to write on their hearts some of the ways we can show love to each other, e.g., helping each other, forgiving each other, being kind to each other, keeping our promises.
3. When you've finished writing down your ideas, lay all the hearts on the table and see how many of these ways Jesus loved us when He died on the cross. He was helping us, forgiving us, being kind, keeping His promise, etc.
4. Glue the heart onto your cross shape if Jesus showed us the kind of love written on the heart when He died on the cross. If the action doesn't quite fit, e.g., doing the dishes, think about the motivation behind the action, such as kindness. Write the motivation on the heart as well, and then stick it onto the cross.
5. Read some of the Bible verses about love that you can find by using a concordance. See if you have missed anything important and add any extra ideas you discover about Jesus' love.

Prayer:

- Thank Jesus for being so willing to die for us.
- Make a thank-You card or a love-You card for Jesus.

Other ideas:

- Look up lots of Bible verses about love. Write each one on a separate heart and stick it onto a larger heart or a cross.
- Fill an attractive jar with your love verses, adding more every time you find a new one. Read the verses whenever you need a special reminder of God's love, or give the jar to someone who is going through a hard time.
- Make a heart-shaped token or object to give to someone. Write "Jesus loves you so much He died for you" on the token or on a tag attached to it.

16

Jesus Died to Save Us Because He Loves Us

The best gift ever! Eternal life—even though we don't deserve it.

Bible connection:
John 3:16. Jesus' death opens the door of heaven for us.

THINGS YOU NEED:

- White cardstock cut into simple person shapes—such as gingerbread men. You will need at least two per person, plus one for Jesus
- A red or white heart of any kind
- A small cross made from scraps of wood, cardstock, or cereal boxes
- Marker pens, pencils, scissors, etc.
- A lovely box or gift bag, preferably gold or white, to illustrate heaven

Worship activities:

1. Read John 3:16. Give everyone a white paper-person shape and ask them to write their name on it. Write "Jesus" on one of the shapes too. Illustrate the story of salvation using these paper shapes.
2. Explain that God loves people so much that He wanted them to live with Him forever and be perfect and happy. (Put your named person shapes into the box or place that illustrates heaven.)
3. When Adam and Eve sinned and sin came into the world, people became hurt and sad. They could no longer live close to God, and they began to die. (Take the paper people out of the box and give them back to their "owners." Ask them to scribble on their person shape and to scrunch it up and tear it.)
4. God knew that unless He did something very special, the people He loved would die forever and never have the opportunity of living with Him.
5. But God still loved them and wanted them to be able to live with Him forever, perfect and happy. So Jesus came and died for all the sins and mistakes we have made. (Place Jesus' shape on the cross shape.)
6. Jesus did this because He loves us so much (place a heart on Jesus on the cross), and because He wanted to take away our sins forever. (Invite each person to place their damaged person underneath the paper Jesus on the cross and receive a new, clean-person shape. Write each person's name on the new shapes.)
7. Now we don't have to die forever, because Jesus died for us. When we believe in Him, we don't have to stay dead forever. He will come and take us to heaven to live with Him always, perfect and happy! (Take the Jesus shape to collect all the "new" people shapes and put them in "heaven.")

Prayer:

- Give everyone their "perfect"-person shape. Invite them to write a prayer of thanks to Jesus for dying for us, so that we don't have to die forever.

Another idea:
- Write each word of John 3:16 on a separate paper-person shape and see how quickly your children can arrange them in order to make the verse.

17

Jesus Died So We Don't Have To!

God completely forgives us whenever we ask Him to.

Bible connection:

"If we confess our sins, he is faithful and just and will forgive us our sins and purify us from all unrighteousness" (1 John 1:9, NIV). All we have to do is confess, and God is more than happy to forgive us because He loves us.

THINGS YOU NEED:

- White modeling compound (commercial product such as Play-Doh or homemade play dough)
- Recipe: mix 2 cups all-purpose flour; 1 cup salt; 2 tablespoons oil; 2 cups water; and 2 tsp. cream of tartar (optional preservative) in a heavy pan.
- Heat gently and keep stirring until the mixture turns gooey. As soon as the mixture starts to come away from the sides of the pan, it's done. Knead well, leave to cool, and keep in an airtight container. (It's important to cook this mixture to just the right texture, or it will be too runny or too stiff to use easily.)

Worship activities:

1. Give each person a lump of modeling compound. Ask them to think quietly about something they have done wrong in the past week and to shape their piece of dough into something that represents their sin.
2. Then ask them to think quietly about what they have done and how it has hurt God, other people, and themselves.
3. Read 1 John 1:9, and tell them that God wants to forgive them completely. As you talk and read, ask them to squish the shape representing the sin into a ball, so that the sin-shape disappears forever. No one can ever take that lump of dough and find out its previous shape. The sin shape has been totally destroyed, just as God destroys all evidence of our sin when we tell Him what we have done and ask Him to forgive us. Psalm 103:8–12.
4. Now talk about how much God loves us, and that nothing can separate us from God's love. As you read Romans 8:38, 39, ask them to shape their ball of dough into a perfect white heart, representing their forgiven heart and God's loving heart. Hold your hearts and thank God for His forgiveness.

Prayer:

- This worship is really a prayer in itself. But you can add to the experience by cutting out a large white heart and asking each person to write a thank-You message to God for His love and forgiveness.

Another idea:

- Blow bubbles to illustrate forgiveness. Ask your children to think of something they have done wrong for which they want to ask God's forgiveness. Then ask them to load their bubble wand with bubble mixture and to blow a stream of bubbles. As they blow the bubbles, they can shut their eyes and ask God to forgive them for their sin. When they open their eyes, the bubbles will have completely disappeared. They cannot be found again and put back into the jar. They have gone forever, just like their sins.

18

We Can Choose to Follow Jesus

God loves us so much that He wants us to have a free choice. He doesn't force us to follow Him if we want to make a different choice.

Bible connection:

"To all who did receive him, to those who believed in his name, he gave the right to become children of God" (John 1:12, NIV). When we believe in Jesus and choose to follow Him, we become God's very own children.

THINGS YOU NEED:

- Gift-wrapped treats that your children will really enjoy, such as a favorite food or a special beverage or a small faith-related gift
- A gold crown for each child, with his name written on it
- Gems and craft supplies to decorate the crowns
- Invitations that say: "Dear child, I hope you will choose to follow Me because I love you and I want you to live with Me in heaven forever."

Worship activities:

1. Find a suitable place to hide the gifts and crowns before worship—preferably in an attractive place.
2. Read John 1:12 and explain what it means—that if we choose to accept Jesus and follow His leadership in our lives, we become children of God.
3. Tell your children that they can choose what to do during worship time. They can do a chore they don't enjoy, without any reward, or they can follow you on an adventure with a treat at the end. Ideally, they'll choose well!
4. Go on a walk through your home, garden, or neighborhood. Go under and over things to make the walk interesting, and into places where your children might not usually go.
5. Ask them to follow you closely and to go wherever you lead them. If you wish you can give them some extra treats along the way, such as a special juice drink or pack of stickers, etc.
6. Finally lead them to the place where you have hidden the crowns and the treats. Crown them as children of God and give them their gifts.
7. Talk about how this activity helps them to understand the choices they are making and the wonderful rewards of choosing to follow God.

Prayer:

- Give each child a handwritten invitation to follow Jesus. Give them the time and space to think about their answer and write it down privately, if they wish. They may also choose to share their answers and choices with you. If this isn't the right time for your children, that's fine. Keep praying, and let the Holy Spirit prepare them for the time that's right for them.

Another idea:

- Download and print the children's version of the "Father's Love Letter," which is a beautiful letter of God's love and an invitation to be His child. http://www.fathersloveletter .com/kids/.

19

Jesus Makes Us New

When we choose to follow Jesus, He changes us! We are new people with different values and priorities.

Bible connection:
"If anyone is in Christ, the new creation has come: The old has gone, the new is here!" (2 Corinthians 5:17, NIV). Once Jesus is in our lives, He changes us from the inside out.

THINGS YOU NEED:
- Books, pictures, video clips, or models illustrating how caterpillars change into butterflies
- Attractive junk, scrap paper, clothespins, chenille wires, colored cellophane, glitter, etc.
- Scissors, adhesive, paper, pens, etc.

Worship activities:
1. Read the Bible verse. It's very exciting that Jesus can change us and make us into new creations! He doesn't just take away our sins and give us clean hearts, but He makes us into princes and princesses and gives us special gifts to help us share His love with others.
2. Show whatever props and pictures you have found to illustrate the way that a caterpillar changes into a butterfly. Look at a picture or model of a caterpillar and a butterfly and list all the differences you can find.
3. Take the junk and craft supplies and invite each person to make a butterfly, using a clothespin, black cardstock, or chenille wire as the body. They can make any design they like, but the wings must be symmetrical and have a heart-motif included in the design.
4. Discuss how different junk looks when it has been turned into butterflies.
5. We may not always feel different when we choose to follow Jesus. We will still make mistakes, but He will always forgive us. The biggest change is that once we choose to follow Jesus and keep following Him, we will not die forever but have everlasting life. John 3:16.
6. Display your butterflies in a special place, or attach them to plain canvas to make interesting wall art. Write the Bible verse on the canvas.

Prayer:
- Let each person use the leftover junk to make something to praise God for loving us enough to transform us and for giving us eternal life.

Another idea:
- Give each person a piece of blotting or watercolor paper. It needs to be at least 8 inches (20 cm) square. Ask them to write their names using water-soluble marker pens about 1 inch (2 cm) above the bottom of the sheet of paper. They can use a different color for each letter in their name, if they wish. Then curve the blotting paper into a cylinder with the letters on the outside. Stand the cylinders in a shallow dish of water and watch the colors rise and blend. Their names will be totally transformed by the water.

20

Jesus Helps Us Grow More Like Him

Jesus knows that the more we become like Him, the happier we'll be. So He wants to help us grow.

Bible connection:

"Jesus grew in wisdom and stature, and in favor with God and man" (Luke 2:52, NIV). We need to keep growing so that we can share more of God's love with those around us.

THINGS YOU NEED:

- A roll of drawing paper or wallpaper, or several sheets of strong paper pasted together to make a long strip
- Green and purple paper with vine leaf and grape templates
- Colored paper, scissors, pencils, marker pens, and glue

Worship activities:

1. Read the Bible verse and talk about how we need to grow to be more like Jesus. Every person, even a grown-up, needs to keep on growing.
2. Make a list of the things that help us to grow more like Jesus, such as reading the Bible, learning about God, listening to God, praying, memorizing scriptures, being kind, developing character strengths, etc.
3. Make a collage of a vine growing up your strip or roll of paper. Cut out lots of green leaves and write on them all the things that help us to grow more like Jesus.
4. Add any Bible verses you can find that will inspire you to grow more like Jesus.
5. Then read about the fruit of the Spirit in Galatians 5:22, 23. Talk about how they show that we're becoming more like Jesus. Cut bunches of grapes from purple paper and write the fruits of the Spirit on them.
6. Add the grapes to the vine collage.
7. Read about character development in 2 Peter 1:5–8, and add these characteristics to your vine.
8. What else shows you are growing more like Jesus? Add these ideas too.

Prayer:

- Invite each person to think of one way he would like to be more like Jesus. Then ask the person on his right to pray for that request, asking God to help him develop the characteristic, wisdom, love, or attitude of Jesus that he hopes and longs for.

Another idea:

- Plant a tomato vine or other easy-to-grow plant. Help your children care for it to remind them of the importance of nurturing their relationship with God. Let them enjoy harvesting and sharing their crops.

SECTION 3

Worships About the Ten Commandments

PUT GOD FIRST

DON'T WORSHIP IDOLS

TREASURE GOD'S NAMES

KEEP GOD'S DAY SPECIAL

RESPECT YOUR PARENTS

PROTECT EACH OTHER

KEEP MARRIAGE SPECIAL

GIVE—DON'T TAKE

SPEAK HONESTLY AND KINDLY

BE CONTENT WITH WHAT YOU HAVE

21

Put God First

When we're Christians, we choose to put God first in our lives. But there are so many distractions. How can we make sure He is truly King of our lives?

Bible connection:

"You shall have no other gods before me" (Exodus 20:3, NIV). When we put God first in our lives, everything else finds perspective and falls into place.

THINGS YOU NEED:

- A plastic container
- A collection of rocks and small stones. One must be much bigger than the others, but it must fit inside the plastic container in such a way that if you don't put it in first, it will be hard to get it in.
- Permanent marker pens and white sticky labels
- Gold cardstock and craft supplies to make and decorate a crown

Worship activities:

1. Read the Bible verse and discuss why God wants us to put Him first in our lives. What happens when we don't put Him first? (We make mistakes, hurt each other, waste our lives, sin, etc.)
2. Take the large rock and let your children write "God" on it. Then pick up the larger stones and write on them the other important things in your life, such as work, school, family, and friends.
3. Pick up the smallest stones and write on them some of the things that can distract us from putting God first, such as TV, computers, games, sports, hobbies, shopping, and following the latest fashions.
4. Take the plastic container and ask your children to put the smallest stones in first. Add all the small stones, even if you haven't written on them. Then add the larger stones, and finally try to fit the "God" rock into the container. Check in advance that it won't fit!
5. Talk about what's wrong. Then fill the container again, putting the "God" rock in first, then add the smaller rocks, and finally the smallest stones.
6. Make a crown together to show that God is King of your lives.
7. As you work on the crown, think about the ways you can make sure God is first in your lives. Write them on the inside of the crown or on sticky labels that can be placed inside the crown.

Prayer:

- Give each person a stone. Pray silently that God will help you let go of the things that prevent Him being first in your lives. Then drop your stones into a garbage can.
- Pass the crown around the circle. Invite each person to pray that God will be King of their lives.

Another idea:

- Write your priorities and distractions on index cards or sticky notes instead of stones. Then work together to arrange them in the order of greatest importance.

22

Don't Worship Idols

Today our idols are not statues made of wood, stone, silver, or clay. But people have many other idols, such as money, fame, fashion, and celebrities. Anything that distracts us from worshiping God can become an idol.

Bible connection:

"You shall not make for yourself an image in the form of anything in heaven above or on the earth beneath or in the waters below. You shall not bow down to them or worship them" (Exodus 20:4, 5, NIV). The biggest problem with idols is that people worship created objects, rather than the Creator of everything.

THINGS YOU NEED:

- Various craft supplies and art materials—whatever you have available
- Images of God and Jesus painted, drawn, and sculpted by different artists; find examples on the Internet and print copies of them

Worship activities:

1. Read the Bible verse and the description of God found in Revelation 4.
2. Look at the pictures and sculptures that artists have created. Which ones do you think look most like the biblical description of God? Which pictures do you like best?
3. Set out the art materials and ask everyone to draw what they think God looks like. Explain that no one has seen God, so we have no real idea what He looks like. But we can imagine what He looks like, or can draw the pictures that we see in our minds when we think of God. Or write descriptions instead.
4. Allow everyone 10 to 15 minutes to work. Then look at what you have drawn.
5. Say, "These are very good pictures! Shall we worship them?" Wait for a response, which will probably be "No!" Then ask why not? (Possible responses: "The drawings are not that good. They're just bits of paper. They can't think or do anything.")
6. Say, "Well, perhaps we should worship each other for making such good pictures of God?" (Possible responses: "No! we shouldn't worship each other because we make mistakes. We can't save each other. Our pictures of God aren't perfect.")
7. Ask, "Whom should we worship?" ("God!" "Why?" "He is real and loving. He created the world. He can do miracles, and He loves and saves us," etc.)
8. Use this activity to help your children understand the foolishness of worshiping and honoring things that people have made—or even things that God has made. Only God is truly worthy of our worship because He is the Power behind all power; the Creator behind all of creation; and the source of all the love in the world.

Prayer:

- Pray around the circle. Start each sentence with: "I worship You, God, because You are . . ."

Another idea:

- Cut large hearts out of paper, preferably red. Write on the hearts all the reasons why it's important to worship God with our whole hearts.

23

Treasure God's Names

God is glorious beyond anything we can imagine. We love Him and want to worship Him, so we show our love and respect by treasuring His names and not using them as swear words or cursing.

Bible connection:

"You shall not misuse the name of the LORD your God, for the LORD will not hold anyone guiltless who misuses His name" (Exodus 20:7, NIV).

THINGS YOU NEED:

- An attractive gift box or a box you can decorate as a treasure box
- Paper in bright, jewel colors
- Pencils, erasers, and scissors
- Templates or patterns for gemstone shapes

Worship activities:

1. Read the Bible verse and talk about why God's names are so special. Talk about why God has so many names. Perhaps He has lots of names because He is important in so many different ways? Why is it so wrong to use His name badly?
2. Think of all the names for God and Jesus that you can remember, and make a list of them.
3. Use a Bible encyclopedia or the Internet to help you.
4. Then use the templates to cut gemstone shapes from the colored paper. Work together to write each of God's names on a different paper gemstone.
5. Make a display of the names on your bulletin board, or gather them up into the treasure chest box, to remind you how precious God's names are.

Prayer:

- Invite each person to choose two or three gemstones with God's names written on them.
- Praise God for each of the special names you have chosen, and for any of His wonderful characteristics that are associated with that name, such as *Savior,* because He saves us, or *Creator,* because He made us.

Other ideas:

- Older children might like to make a poster of some of God's names using a Web site like http://www.wordle.net or another creative design program.
- Discuss polite and respectful ways your children can encourage their friends not to use God's name badly in their conversations.

Keep God's Day Special

Sabbath is a gift from God—a gift we can open and enjoy every single week. It's a gift of time to spend loving Him and loving each other.

Bible connection:

Exodus 20:8–11; Isaiah 58:13, 14. God wants us to have a delightful day every week, so that we can worship Him, love Him, and care for each other. How can we make our Sabbaths more delightful?

THINGS YOU NEED:

- An attractive gift bag
- A collection of items that illustrate various aspects of Sabbath, such as a rechargeable battery; soothing hand lotion; a sparkling "gem"; a small heart; a packet of tissues; a small candle; a box of raisins; a small bottle of perfume; a smiley face; a doll's pillow; a book about nature; a Band-Aid; bottle of drinking water or carton of juice; etc. Put all of these items into the gift bag.
- Sticky notes and pens

Worship activities:

1. Read the Bible verses about Sabbath.
2. Tell your children that Sabbath is a special gift from God to us that we can open every week. He made it for our happiness and enjoyment, for rest, and for spending time loving Him and loving each other.
3. Take turns putting your hand into the gift bag, without looking, and pulling out an object. Talk about how each item can help us understand more about the gift of the Sabbath as a day for refreshing, healing, loving, soothing, recharging our batteries, etc. It's also a beautiful and precious day.
4. Write on the sticky notes all the gifts from God that we can find in the gift of the Sabbath. Stick them onto one side of the gift bag.
5. Then read the text about Sabbath being a delight. Think of all the delightful things your family has done on Sabbath. Write them on sticky notes to remind you to do them more often. Add your other ideas for making Sabbath a delight. Stick these on the other side of the gift bag.
6. Make a plan for a special Sabbath in the future. What will you do? Where will you go? With whom will you share God's love? etc.

Prayer:

- Pass the gift bag you have created around the circle as you pray. Thank God for His gift of delightful Sabbaths.

Another idea:

- Print certificate blanks or design your own certificates for "The Best Sabbath Ever" award. Include the date, place, and what you did that made it so special. Let each person complete their own certificates for their best Sabbath ever. Plan to do more of the delightful things that your family enjoys doing on Sabbath.

25

Respect Your Parents

Respect is about honoring and treasuring other people and showing them how special they are to us and to God. When we treat people with respect, we all benefit; when we disrespect others, we all suffer.

Bible connection:

"Honor your father and your mother" (Exodus 20:12, NIV). See also Romans 12:10. It's important to respect our family members, especially our parents who have given us life and taken care of us.

THINGS YOU NEED:

- Large circles (draw around a saucer or small plate) cut from white or yellow/gold poster board or the inside of white cereal boxes—enough for each person in the family to make one for everyone else
- Hole punch
- Lengths of ribbon, yarn, or twine
- Marker pens, pencils, and scissors

Worship activities:

1. Read the Bible verses. Talk about times when each of you felt respected, honored, or blessed by someone else in your family, such as when they helped you, obeyed you, were thoughtful and considerate, etc.
2. Talk about what respect and honor means—saying and doing things that lift the other person up and make them feel happy and special, rather than putting them down and making them feel sad and lonely.
3. Discuss why God thought that honoring parents was so important that He included it in the commandments. (When we honor our parents, we are also honoring God; when we honor and obey our parents, we learn to show God respect and obedience too.)
4. Sometimes people are shown honor and respect by receiving medals recognizing their courage, excellence, hard work, etc.
5. Punch a hole in each circle and make it into a medal by threading yarn, etc. through the hole.
6. Give each person enough "medals" to make one for everyone else. Use marker pens to draw designs and write honoring words on the medals.
7. Hold a small presentation ceremony, honoring each person in turn, placing medals around their necks, making short speeches, and cheering for them.

Prayer:

- After each person has been honored, hold hands in a circle around them, thank God for them, and bless them.

Another idea:

- Invite your children to make a list of ways to show respect in your family. Turn their ideas into an attractive and appealing poster.

26

Protect Each Other

Although most of us are very unlikely to murder anyone, this commandment reminds us to take care of each other, protect each other, and be gentle with each other, because life and people are fragile.

Bible connection:

"You shall not murder" (Exodus 20:13, NIV). Our lives are a special gift from God. When we help to protect each other, we are showing God's love.

THINGS YOU NEED:

- A collection of things that protect people or objects (egg carton, ear plugs, mitten, boot, pot holders, goggles, cycle helmet, shoes, sunscreen, insect repellent, bicycle lamps, etc.)
- Paper and pencils
- Index cards or paper with the following types of scenarios written on them: a small child is being bullied; a friend wants to ride a bike without wearing a cycle helmet; a friend suggests playing a dangerous game; a child is too close to a river or a busy road; a toddler wants to eat some poisonous berries; an adult suddenly collapses onto the floor; a younger brother squirms out of his car-seat straps; etc. Choose situations where your child could realistically help to protect others.

Worship activities:

1. Read the Bible verse. Explain that this verse encourages us to protect each other from harm.
2. Look at each of the protective items you have gathered. They have all been designed to keep people or things safe from heat, water, noise, cold, damage, etc. Explore the different ways they offer protection and how they have been especially designed to protect people and objects.
3. God has designed us to protect each other and not to hurt each other.
4. Read the scenario cards together and talk about the realistic and practical things your children could do to protect others from being hurt, bullied, or teased. Write your ideas down on the paper or cards.
5. Invite younger children to draw pictures of the people who protect us, such as firemen, policemen, doctors, nurses, teachers, and parents.
6. God protects us in many ways, and when we protect others, we show other people His love.

Prayer:

- Write thank-You prayers for God's protection on egg-shaped pieces of paper and place them in an open egg carton. Write "Thank You, God, for protecting us!" on the lid.

Another idea:

- Tell your children stories of the times when God protected you, or them, in a special way. These stories will encourage their faith in a loving and protecting God.

Keep Marriage Special

God wants us to keep our marriages special so that families are kept safe and happy, and so that we can understand how much He loves us.

Bible connection:

"You shall not commit adultery" (Exodus 20:14, NIV). God wants us to keep our marriage promises and cherish each other, just as He has promised to take care of us and cherish us. Marriage is a symbol of God's dedicated relationship with His people. It also illustrates His desire for us to be totally committed to Him. See also Ephesians 5:21–33.

THINGS YOU NEED:

- Pictures, albums, and videos of family weddings
- Several white hearts cut from sturdy white paper or cardstock
- Very strong glue, marker pens
- A copy of wedding vows

Worship activities:

1. Read Exodus 20:14 and Ephesians 5:21–33.
2. Look at your family wedding photos and tell special stories about the weddings and the happy marriages in your family.
3. Talk about marriage being very important because it is a living illustration of the relationship between God and us.
4. Take two hearts and write "God" on one and "Us" on the other. Stick the blank sides together with very strong glue. You may need to prepare one of these a day before the worship, so the adhesive can set well.
5. God is glued to us with the strongest glue ever—His love. When we wander away from Him or reject Him, we become damaged and hurt, and He hurts too. Ask your children to tear the "Us" heart away from the "God" heart and show how each heart is damaged and hurt.
6. Repeat the activity, writing "Husband" on one heart and "Wife" on the other. Before you glue the hearts together in "marriage," read aloud the wedding vows and have the hearts "say" the vows to each other.
7. Then glue them together or produce a pair you "bonded" the day before.
8. Ask your children what will happen if you pull these two apart. What will each of them feel? What might their children feel if their marriage is torn apart? What will their friends feel? And what will God feel? Why are happy and strong marriages so important to Him and to us?

Prayer:

- Pray that God will bless and strengthen the marriages in your family.
- Pray that your children will be dedicated, loving spouses in the future and find dedicated, loving partners.

Another idea:

- If your children enjoy being creative or dressing up, hold an improvised wedding. Dress the bride and groom in things you can find around the house. Celebrate with a piece of cake and a drink of juice!

28

Give—Don't Take

God is very generous with each of us, and He wants us to be generous with others. When we're generous, we are showing others God's love.

Bible connection:

"You shall not steal" (Exodus 20:15, NIV). When we take things away from people, it hurts them and makes them feel sad and afraid. When we share with them, they feel happy and loved.

THINGS YOU NEED:
- A box of variously colored toy bricks (such as Legos)
- Small prize—one for each person (optional)
- A current local newspaper

Worship activities:
1. Make a simple stand-up heart shape from red bricks. Place it on a base in the middle of the table so everyone can see it.
2. Give each person a set of red bricks so they can copy the heart, but give everyone one less brick than they need.
3. Tell everyone to copy the heart model exactly, without speaking and without touching the heart. Offer a small prize for the first person to complete his or her heart, if you wish.
4. Watch what happens when people realize that they don't enough bricks. Do they try to take someone else's piece? If they ask you for an extra piece, happily and generously give them the piece they need.
5. Stop the activity before people start to get cross with each other! Give everyone the bricks they need, and then give everyone a small prize.
6. Discuss how each person would have felt, or did feel, if someone had taken one of their pieces.
7. Do the activity again. Ask each person to find enough bricks of one color to make the heart model, and then (generously) give them to another member of the family so they can make a different heart.
8. Stand your brick hearts on a base. Keep them on display for a week to remind everyone that giving happily, instead of taking, shows God's love.

Prayer:
- Look through your local newspaper for stories of people who have had things stolen from them. Pray for them, that God will provide the things they need; and pray for those who stole, that they will stop taking things and will return the stolen goods to their owners.
- Send a card or a small gift to someone who has experienced a burglary. Let them know that you care and that you are praying for them.

Another idea:
- Make a sunshine kit to give to someone. Fill it with sunny and cheerful things, such as a potted daisy or pansy, a box of Bible promises, roasted sunflower seeds, orange juice, a handmade card, etc.

29

Speak Honestly and Kindly

Words can build people up and tear them down. Lies are especially hurtful because they can hurt relationships and cause all kinds of damage.

Bible connection:

"You shall not give false testimony against your neighbor" (Exodus 20:16, NIV). See also Ephesians 4:29. Words are very powerful, and we need to use them thoughtfully and lovingly.

THINGS YOU NEED:

- Large sheet of paper. Draw a large heart on your sheet of paper. It needs to be big enough to contain 10 to 12 brick shapes.
- Grey/brown paper cut into brick shapes
- Marker pens
- Glue stick
- Speech bubbles cut from copy paper

Worship activities:

1. Read the Bible verses and talk about the kind things people have said to you this week that encouraged you and made you feel happy inside.
2. Write these kind words on some of the paper bricks. Write on the bricks other kind things that people might say, too.
3. Then think about the unkind and lying words people say. Instead of writing the actual unkind words, write category words, such as criticism, bullying, teasing, lying, put-downs, discouragement, or cruel words.
4. Shuffle your "bricks" and place them upside down in a pile. Take turns picking up a brick and deciding whether it's garbage and needs to go in the garbage can, or if it contains loving words that build people up. Glue the loving words onto the heart shape to make a strong brick-wall pattern, because loving words build us up.

Prayer:

- Cut speech bubbles out of paper. Write prayers on them, asking God to help you say kind and encouraging things, and not hurtful words.

Other ideas:

- Give everyone a sheet of paper or a notebook. Ask them to say at least three kind things a day to the people around them and to write what they say in their notebooks. Ask them to note the effect that their words had on the other person, e.g., they smiled; did nothing; said "Thank you!"; or showed that they appreciated the kind words.
- Give your children some attractive writing paper and invite them to write a lovely letter to a grandparent or other family member.

45

30

Be Content With What You Have

Most of the advertising we see is designed to make us feel discontented and to want more than we have. But God wants us to trust Him to provide for our needs, and He wants us to be happy with the things we have.

Bible connection:

"You shall not covet" (Exodus 21:17, NIV). Coveting means wanting what other people have, rather than being content with the treasures God has already given us. See also Philippians 4:2. The happiest people in the world are not those who *have* the most— they are those who *give* the most away.

THINGS YOU NEED:

- A stack of catalogs and magazines
- Scissors and adhesive
- Paper and pencils

Worship activities:

1. Read the Bible verses and explain what *covet* means. Discuss why God is so concerned about coveting that He included it in His commandments. Why is it wrong for us to want what other people have? How might it lead us to break some of the other commandments? And how does it spoil our own happiness?
2. Make a list of the wrong or unwise things people do when they covet something— steal, hurt others, buy things they don't need, spend too much money, work long hours and neglect their families, etc.
3. Make a list of the good things to do or think about when it's tempting to covet. (Think about the good things you already have, thank God for what you have, make the most of the things you already own, etc.)
4. Give everyone a catalog or a magazine and ask them to find 10 different things that they are glad they don't own. Ask them to glue the pictures onto a sheet of paper and write why they're glad they don't have any of these things.
5. Then look at your collections. What's the funniest thing you found that you're glad you don't have?

Prayer:

- Thank God for all the things that you're glad you don't have! Ask God to help you be contented with the hundreds of gifts He has already given you.

Other ideas:

- Start a sentence with phrases like: "I'm content with the food I ate today because . . ." "I'm content with the pair of shoes I wore today because . . ." "I'm content with the clothes in my wardrobe because . . ." Then let each person complete the sentence in their own words.
- Create a rule that anyone who whines for something has to list 20 things they're thankful for.

SECTION 4

Worships Exploring Bible Stories

31

Acrostic Bible Stories

This is a fun and challenging activity that involves thinking creatively about various Bible characters. It's also a good game for long journeys and the days when you have to stay indoors.

Bible connection:

"Abraham was a hundred years old when his son Isaac was born to him. Sarah said, 'God has brought me laughter, and everyone who hears about this will laugh with me' " (Genesis 21:5, 6, NIV). In Bible times children were given names that had special meanings or that told stories about them. See if you can tell stories about various Bible characters by using their names to help you.

THINGS YOU NEED:

- Paper, pens, and pencils

Worship activities:

1. Talk about the names of each person in your family. Why was each name chosen? What do your names mean?
2. Explain that in Bible times many names had special meanings. Look up the meanings of a few Bible names. See who can find the most unusual meaning of a name, such as those of Hosea's children (Hosea 1:3–9).
3. Then let each person choose a Bible character and create a short description or story about them using the letters of their name as an acrostic. That means each word will begin with the letters of the name, in order. You can also add a few extra short words, to help you out.
   - PAUL—Preacher, Ambassador, Upholder of the faith, Letter writer
   - NAOMI—Nice, Amiable, Old, Mother-In-Law
   - RUTH—Refugee, Untiring, Trusting, Helper
   - ABRAM—Adventurer, Believing Rightly About Messiah

   Write down the names and your acrostic descriptions. Add more to your list as you think of them.

Prayer:

- Praise God for 26 of His characteristics and names, finding at least one for each letter of the alphabet in turn. It's possible to find one for every letter, including Q and Z (Quick, Quieting, Quenching, Zealous, etc.)

Other ideas:

- Make acrostic stories for your own names, creating encouraging and positive descriptions of each other.
- Or create a slogan using the letters of your surname/family name as an acrostic. E.g., HOLFORD—Happy Ones, Living Faithfully, Optimistic, Redeemed, and Devoted.

The Ark Challenge

God gave Noah the design to build the ark and save all the animals. The Bible tells us what it looked like on the outside, but what was it like on the inside?

Bible connection:

Genesis 6:11–21. God told Noah to build the ark with three stories of rooms in it and spaces for all the animals, his family, and all their food.

THINGS YOU NEED:

- Picture books of Noah's ark
- Toy animals, animal picture cards, or pictures of animals drawn on paper
- Construction toys, small boxes, old cereal boxes, and shoeboxes
- Large sheets of paper, pencils, eraser, marker pens, etc.
- Several sheets of cardstock

Worship activities:

1. Read the story of Noah's ark. Compare any pictures you have of the ark. Which ones look most like the description in Genesis 6?
2. Imagine you are Noah building the ark. What would you need to think about? How would you house the giraffes, lions, elephants, mice, birds, alligators, rabbits, butterflies, etc.? What space would each need? How would they get water and food? How would you keep them safe? How much food would you need to feed all those animals for so many months? Where would you put the food to keep it safe and have easy access to it? What about the animals' bedding and cleaning all the cages?
3. Talk about your ideas and how Noah might have solved some of these challenges, such as designing food and water chutes; making a space on each floor where he could empty all the waste; or putting similar animals together, such as sheep, goats, cows, and horses.
4. Draw a plan, or construct some animal pens, to see if you can work out good ways to look after all the animals on the ark. Use the animals, cards, boxes, and other materials to help you.
5. How do you imagine God helped Noah? Maybe some animals hibernated or needed less water or were more docile? Maybe all the animals ate grains for the entire journey. God was protecting them all in a special way.

Prayer:

Fold a sheet of cardstock in half and cut out a simple ark shape keeping the fold at the top of the roof. Talk about the important lessons you have learned from the story of Noah's ark and use them to inspire your prayers. Write your prayers on the ark cards. Thank God for His amazing protection and pray for the character strengths that Noah developed, such as patience, perseverance, creativity, resourcefulness, and kindness.

Another idea:

Imagine you are Noah's wife. Write the story of Noah's ark from her perspective. Write a few of her journal entries, or write about a day in the life of the floating ark.

33

Story Rolls

Help your children make story rolls to tell their favorite Bible stories. They can be rolled up and popped into a small bag with a story book and a few small objects or pictures.

Bible connection:

Choose your Bible story and read it in a translation your children enjoy or from a well-written Bible storybook. Or find a good video clip of the story on the Internet or at http://www.gracelink.net.

THINGS YOU NEED:

- Strips of colored felt, about 5 to 6 inches (15 cm) wide and about 3 feet (1 m) long
- Small items, toys, pictures, and shapes that represent items mentioned in the story, such as sheep, a shepherd, cut yarn for grass, and a blue ribbon for water.
- A small basket filled with items and pictures of items mentioned in the story, placed next to the unrolled strip of felt.
- You can also use a roll of paper and marker pens

Worship activities:

1. Read your chosen Bible story. As you tell the story, ask your children to find the items mentioned in the story and lay them on the felt story roll.
2. Repeat this process a couple of times and then ask your children to tell the story to you, placing the items on the felt roll as they speak.
3. Make a set of these story rolls and keep them in little bags, together with all the pieces. Include a suitable book, so that your children can tell themselves the Bible stories and play with the pieces.
4. Older children can create something similar on rolls of drawing paper or on the back of an unused roll of wallpaper. As you tell the story, they can draw quick doodles and pictures of the events, or of the items you mention, to create a cartoon, or a story "road." They can also help find items to place on the wallpaper story roll to tell the story.

Prayer:

- Write or draw your family prayer on a roll of paper.
- Divide a length of paper roll into four sections:
    1. We praise You God because . . . (praise prayers)
    2. We thank You God for . . . (prayers of thanks)
    3. We're sorry that we . . . (prayers for forgiveness)
    4. Please help . . . (prayer requests)
- Let everyone move around the paper, adding sentences, pictures, and objects to illustrate their prayers.
- Writing on the roll together is praying, but you can also read out what has been written in the different sections if you wish.

Another idea:

- Older children can make story rolls and bags for the younger children in the family or as gifts for the younger children at church.

Sensory Stories

God wants us to experience and worship Him using our whole bodies, including our senses. The tabernacle services and many of the Jewish festivals were packed with smells, sights, sounds, flavors, and textures.

Bible connection:

"Taste and see that the LORD is good" (Psalm 34:8, NIV). God has given us five amazing senses so that we can experience His goodness and wonder.

THINGS YOU NEED:

- A suitable Bible story with tastes and sounds, etc. You can find several sensory experiences for most Bible stories
- A collection of sound makers, textures, Bible story objects, things to taste and smell, etc.
- Small containers for keeping the objects safely stored
- A sturdy box

Worship activities:

1. Read the Bible verse and talk about how we can taste, smell, feel, hear, and see God's goodness. Talk about the things you have experienced in the past day that have helped you to taste and see His goodness.
2. Lay out a few sensory experiences as they occur in the Bible story you have chosen. Let your children smell perfumes, bread, grape juice, grains, leather, etc. Have them touch wood, stones, water, the breeze of a fan (wind), feathers, clay pots, linen, animal skins, etc. They can also taste honey, bread, grape juice, milk, popped corn (roasted grain), raisins, almonds, etc. Let them shake small plastic bottles filled with sand, gravel, water, and stones to simulate people walking on a variety of surfaces, or visiting the well, etc.; clap castanets or coconut shells to make the sound of animals' feet on the ground; or blow bird-sound whistles; or play Bible instruments such as horns, tambourines, bells, harps, etc. Have them look at rainbows, gems, gold objects, clay lamps, toy animals, etc.
3. Place any nonperishable objects in your sturdy sensory box and use them to add sensory dimensions to your Bible stories. Be creative about looking for new things to add, and involve your children in the hunt.
4. How do the Bible story you have just heard and the senses you have experienced help you to taste and see God's love and greatness?

Prayer:

- Praise God for your senses. Invite everyone to thank God for their favorite sounds, sights, smells, textures, and tastes.

Another idea:

- Start your sensory box by sending your children on a scavenger hunt to find sensory items in your home that remind them of a Bible story or verse. Show each other what you found and try to guess the connection. Save any suitable sensory items in your box to use during other worships.

35

An Any-Story Worship

There are times when you're busy and out of ideas and energy for family worship. This is a simple format for your family to explore any Bible story.

Bible connection:

"All Scripture is God-breathed and is useful for teaching, rebuking, correcting and training in righteousness, so that the servant of God may be thoroughly equipped for every good work" (2 Timothy 3:16, 17, NIV). This approach to exploring a Bible story can be inspiring for children and adults of all ages.

THINGS YOU NEED:

- A Bible story
- A few simple props or pictures, or a good book or video clip of the story
- A neat assortment of quality craft materials, scissors, adhesives, etc.

Worship activities:

1. Tell the Bible story in your favorite interactive way.
2. Use simple props, such as felts and little objects, to illustrate your stories.
3. When you have finished telling the story, ask the following questions: (There are no right or wrong answers, so create an atmosphere in which your children's simple and imaginative ideas are accepted and discussed freely.)
4. What's your favorite part of the story?
5. What do you think are the most important messages in the story?
6. What does this story tell you about God's love and His character?
7. What does this story inspire you to do for God or someone else?
8. Once you have all shared your ideas, let everyone choose how they'd like to immediately respond to the story. They can write a story, poem, or letter to God; they can create something out of the craft materials to remind them of the story; or they can prepare or plan a kind action inspired by the story.
9. Come back together after 15 minutes and talk about how the story has inspired you.

Prayer:

- Take turns thanking God for whatever the story has inspired you to do, or for anything new the story has taught you about Him.

Other ideas:

- When you're tired or busy, try giving your children a Bible story to tell to the rest of the family in any way they like. Choose a simple story, such as a parable or Noah's ark. Allow half an hour for them to plan and find what they need.
- Keep everything you need for a last-minute worship activity in a bag or box so that you can create a last-minute worship on a busy day.

36

Feeling Stories

Exploring other people's emotions, in familiar Bible stories, can help your children widen their own emotional vocabulary.

Bible connection:

"An angel of the Lord appeared to [the shepherds], and the glory of the Lord shone around them, and they were terrified. But the angel said to them, 'Do not be afraid. I bring you good news that will cause great joy for all the people' " (Luke 2:9, 10, NIV). What emotions do you think the shepherds experienced during the wonderful night that Jesus was born?

THINGS YOU NEED:

• Paper and pens

Worship activities:

1. Read the Bible verses and imagine what it was like to be a shepherd on the Bethlehem hills the night that Jesus was born. We know from the story that they were frightened by the angels and then happy and excited as they ran into town to find Jesus. What other feelings might they have had?
2. Take several sheets of paper and write one of the following words on each sheet: Confused, Worried, Sad, Angry, Afraid, Happy.
3. Then think of as many feeling words as you can, and write each feeling under the heading on one of the sheets of paper, or start a new category. This will give you a rich choice of feelings.
4. Keep your feeling lists and add other emotions as you think of them.
5. Stay with the story of Jesus' birth, and think about the feelings the various characters in the story experienced: Mary and Joseph, the innkeeper, God, the angels, the wise men, and Herod.
6. Make a list of all the feelings each person may have had during the story.
7. Talk about why God made us with feelings. (Fear can protect us; happiness helps us to enjoy life; anger can help us to stand up for ourselves or protect someone who is vulnerable; sadness is a natural response when we've lost something precious to us; our feelings help us to communicate with each other and care for each other, etc.)

Prayer:

• Pray about your feelings. (Thank You that I am feeling happy about . . . ; I am feeling sad about ...; please comfort me; I am feeling angry about ...; please calm me and give me wisdom; I am worried/afraid about . . . ; please help me to trust You to sort out the problem; etc.)

Other ideas:

• Play a feeling game by calling out an emotion and having each person list all the people in the Bible who were happy, sad, angry, afraid, etc. See who can list the most, or work on this activity together.
• Talk about what to do in your family if you are feeling sad, afraid, worried, angry, etc. How can you talk about your feelings, and how can you respond to other people who are experiencing some of these various emotions?

37

Cartoon-Drawing Stories

Some children and teenagers enjoy visual stories. Try making Bible-story cartoon drawings (comic-strip style) to stimulate their creativity and interest.

Bible connection:
Read a favorite and active Bible story.

THINGS YOU NEED:
- Paper, pencils, pens, erasers, rulers, etc.
- An assortment of comic strips—some based on Bible stories—to show a variety of cartoon styles and designs.

Worship activities:
1. Read your chosen Bible story.
2. Invite everyone to retell the story in their own way.
3. Suggest that they might like to create cartoons to tell the story. Look at the sample comic strips to see how they are constructed and designed, and the difference between thought bubbles and speech bubbles, etc.
4. Also suggest that some might like to rewrite the story as a poem or in their own words, because not everyone likes to draw.
5. Allow 15 minutes for everyone to work on their stories. Explain that stick figures and simple drawings are good for creating a rough plan for the comic strip. If they enjoy working on it and want to improve the pictures, they can continue after worship.
6. Come back together as a family to show and read your stories.

Prayer:
- Create a cartoon-drawing prayer. Invite each person to draw four pictures, illustrating why they want to praise God, thank Him, ask forgiveness, and make a request.
- Cut out the pictures and place all the praise pictures in a row; then the thankfulness prayers, etc.
- Read out your cartoon prayer or glue it onto a background and create a poster.

Other ideas:
- Divide the story into different frames or sections and invite each person to write and illustrate one or two frames of the story or comic strip. Then assemble them together.
- Invite older children to create Bible story comic strips to illustrate Bible stories for the younger children in their family or church.

38

Bible Character Explorer Book

Create small books that explore the lives of your favorite Bible characters.

Bible connection:

Hebrews 11 lists many Bible heroes and examples of their faith. The stories of these heroes can inspire our faith too.

THINGS YOU NEED:

- Four sheets of paper folded in half and stapled or stitched to make a small book
- Scissors, pens, pencils, erasers
- Marker pens or crayons

Worship activities:

1. Create a story book with eight pages as follows:
   - Front cover: "The Story of . . ." add the name of the Bible character and draw a picture of him or her on the front cover.
   - Page 1: Write any special stories of the person's birth or family, a drawing of their family tree, or a map showing where they lived, etc.
   - Page 2: List or draw some happy things that happened to the Bible character.
   - Page 3: Write about a mistake the Bible character made, or that someone else in the story made.
   - Page 4: Write about a challenge that he or she faced, and how God helped him or her to manage the challenge.
   - Page 5: Write a list of the person's character strengths, such as faith, courage, perseverance, kindness, or generosity.
   - Page 6: Write what this person's life has taught you about God's love.
   - Back cover: This book was created by . . . (write your own name)
2. Let each person make a book like this about his or her favorite Bible character, filling it with stories and pictures.
3. When you have finished, show each other your storybooks and read what each has written.
4. Discuss what new things have you learned about these Bible characters and what new things have you learned about their faith through doing this activity.

Prayer:

- Use the general outline of the book above as a guide for your prayers: thank God for the happy events, ask forgiveness for your mistakes, ask God to help you with your challenges, and thank God for the character strengths you have noticed in each other's lives during the past week.

Another idea:

- Use the page layout above as a guide to write your individual faith-story books. Change some of the page themes to include answered prayers, etc.

39

Don't Mention It!

This is a simple, fun Bible game that is ideal for playing in the car when you're traveling.

Bible connection:

"Those who guard their lips preserve their lives, but those who speak rashly will come to ruin" (Proverbs 13:3, NIV). This is a fun way to help children think carefully about what they say.

THINGS YOU NEED:

- 20 or more index cards
- Paper and pens
- A timer
- Pile of buttons or other small tokens
- Honey or other sweet liquid

Prepare for this activity by writing the title of a Bible story at the top of each index card. Then list six key words from the story on the card. For example:

Noah's Ark, boat, rain, animals, rainbow, dove, flood

Worship activities:

1. Read the Bible verse and talk about the importance of choosing our words carefully, so that they are kind and encouraging.
2. Then introduce the Bible game. Place the cards face down in the middle of the group. Take turns picking up the top card of the pack and laying it face up on the table. The person who turned over the card has one minute to tell the story on the card, without using any of the listed and "forbidden" words.
3. Each time anyone says a "forbidden" word, they are given a button.
4. After a minute they stop telling their story, and the next person picks up a card.
5. Stop the game before the youngest child becomes bored with it, or let each person take two or three turns.
6. Talk about how hard it is to stop yourself from saying certain words, and how challenging it is to think more carefully about what you are saying.
7. How can we choose our words more carefully so they are more loving?

Prayer:

- Place a drop of honey on each person's tongue and ask them to keep it there while you pray. Pray that all your words will be "sweet" for others to hear and that they will "taste" kind, encouraging, true, and helpful, etc.

Another idea:

- In Bible times honey was used to help children learn Bible verses. The teacher wrote the verse and then spread honey over the words. The children would trace the words with their fingertips and then lick the honey off their fingers. Print or write a Bible verse using large letters. Put it inside a clear plastic bag, and spread honey over it. Then let your children trace the words and enjoy the honey. Proverbs 16:24; Psalm 119:103.

40

Where in the Bible?

Challenge your children to think of the different Bible stories that mention familiar objects.

Bible connection:

"Does not the potter have the right to make out of the same lump of clay some pottery for special purposes and some for common use?" (Romans 9:21, NIV). Even though we may think we are quite ordinary, God has plans to weave us into His amazing stories.

THINGS YOU NEED:

- Paper and pens
- A stack of plain index cards
- A buzzing timer
- Preparation: Make a list of items mentioned in several Bible stories, such as a donkey, a well, a river, a pot, a fire, fish, birds, wood, seas, a boat or ship, stones, sheep, perfume, bread, a snake, a coin, a lamp, a basket, an inn, a tree. Write each word on a separate card.

Worship activities:

1. Read the Scripture reading and talk about how God likes to weave us into His special plans. Explain that even though your family may own special dishes, they're usually stored away safely. It's the plain and simple dishes you use every day that are the most useful!
2. Give each player a sheet of paper and a pen. Place the cards face down on the table.
3. Turn over one card at a time and set the timer for 30 seconds. Adjust the timer to suit your children's concentration and abilities.
4. Give everyone 30 seconds to write a list of all the Bible stories they can remember that include the object on the card. Then turn over a new card and reset the timer. Work in teams to support younger children.
5. Or play cooperatively by working together to name as many Bible stories as you can.

Prayer:

- Turn all the cards face up and let each person choose an object that illustrates something they'd like to do for God. For example, I'd like to be a sheep and just follow You, I'd like to be a bottle of perfume and make the world fragrant with Your love.
- Pray that God will use each of you in the special way you have chosen.

Another idea:

- Play a variation of the game by turning all the cards face down and spreading them on the table. Take turns turning over two cards at a time. If the player can name a Bible story that clearly mentions both items, they can keep the cards and have another turn. There may be some cards at the end of the game that can't be paired.

SECTION 5

Worships Involving Creativity

41

Bible Trophies

Design or make unique trophies for the special heroes in the Bible, and perhaps for the special heroes in your own family.

Bible connection:

Hebrews 11. When we read through this chapter, we can see that by faith some people did simple things, and by faith some accomplished more challenging things for God. But it was God who helped each of these heroes to make a difference and to carry out His plans for His people.

THINGS YOU NEED:

- Paper, pencils, glue, and scissors
- Junk, craft materials, and things you have around the home

Worship activities:

1. Who are your Bible heroes? Who else could Paul have included in his faith-hero list if he had had more time and space?
2. Make a list of some of the other faith heroes and heroines in the Bible. Don't forget the less obvious ones, such as Dorcas or the little boy who gave his lunch to Jesus.
3. Have everyone choose their favorite Bible hero or heroine and think how God worked through their faith to do amazing things.
4. Design trophies or awards for your favorite faith heroes or heroines.
5. Draw your trophies on paper. Think about the best designs to suit the recipients' accomplishments. Also write some words on their trophies that celebrate their incredible faith in God, because that's how they did amazing things.
6. Make trophies for your faith heroes out of junk and things you can find around the house. Cut the top off an empty soda bottle and turn it upside down to make a cup shape. Or use an old foil tray to create a silver platter and "engrave" it by pressing hard with an old ball-point pen over a cork surface. Or build a trophy from your construction toys.
7. Cut words for your trophy from old newspapers, or print them on your computer. Decorate your creations with a layer of tissue paper, plastic cut from plastic bags, or odds and ends you no longer need.
8. When you have finished your trophies, hold a mini celebration and imagine you are presenting your trophies to your faith heroes.

Prayer:

- Make a praise trophy for God to thank Him for using His amazing power to help His people down through the ages.
- Thank God for the stories of your favorite faith heroes and ask God to strengthen your faith so He can do amazing things through you too.

Another idea:

- Invite everyone to search for things that would make good trophies for each of the other people in your family. Perhaps a wooden spoon would make a trophy for the best cook in the family, or a screwdriver for the best "fix it" person. Thank God for each other's gifts and strengths.

42

A Song for You

Parents often make up songs to sing about their children. God loves us so much that He delights in us, and He also sings wonderful songs of joy over us.

Bible connection:

"The LORD your God is with you.... He will take great delight in you; in His love He will ...rejoice over you with singing" (Zephaniah 3:17, NIV). What song do you think God is singing over you today?

THINGS YOU NEED:

- Paper
- Pencils
- Worship CDs and CD player (optional)

Worship activities:

1. Read the Bible verse above and imagine God delighting in you and singing over you.
2. Does your family have its own little songs you sing together, or about each other, in a loving and delightful way? What songs did you sing over your children when they were small or trying to go to sleep?
3. Imagine the different songs God might be singing over each of you today. Maybe one of you needs a comforting song, a celebrating song, or a lively song to keep you working at a difficult task.
4. Maybe God has a different song for each of us. Maybe He sings different verses of it depending on what we need. Talk about the kind of songs you most need God to sing over you today.
5. Choose a tune you all know and enjoy. Make up a verse for each person, matching the words to their needs. Then sing the verses to, or "over," each other.

Prayer:

- Sing your prayers to God. What song would you most like to sing for God today? Choose songs or hymns that express what you want to say to God. Sing a verse from each song, or listen to the songs prayerfully.

Other ideas:

- Older children might like to choose pieces of music that illustrate various aspects of God's character.
- Make up a family theme song together, one that you can sing when you want to call everyone to worship. Use a tune that everyone knows well so you can concentrate on writing the words. Or let each person write a different verse for your family song.

43

Heavenly City

Work together to create an imaginary model of the New Jerusalem in heaven.

Bible connection:

Revelation 21:1–3, 9–27. The description of the New Jerusalem sounds incredibly beautiful. Make your own model of the heavenly city using craft materials. Talk about heaven as you work together.

THINGS YOU NEED:

* Thick lining paper to make the base/street layout of your city
* Lots of scraps in all kinds of shapes and sizes—cardstock, plastic, fabric, paper, craft supplies, wool, string, paper fasteners, straws, popsicle sticks, etc.
* Glue and tapes
* Paints and marker pens
* Scissors, etc.

Worship activities:

1. Read the beautiful description of the New Jerusalem.
2. Think about the wonderful colors, glittering stones, and gleaming gold that will be all around the city.
3. Imagine what there will be in the city—parks, flowers, trees, beautiful homes, places to meet each other, etc. What might we do in heaven, and what else might be in the city?
4. Use your imagination while remembering that heaven will be beyond anything we can ever imagine!
5. Draw a street layout for your city, thinking about the shape of the city and its twelve pearl gates. Then fill the streets with houses, buildings, parks, trees, etc. Add any toy animals and people you can find.
6. What are each of you most looking forward to doing and seeing in heaven?

Prayer:

* Thank God for making heaven such a wonderful place to be. Take turns telling God why you want to go to heaven and be with Him forever.
* Hold hands and pray that you'll all be ready to go to heaven when Jesus comes again.

Other ideas:

* Make your heavenly model in miniature using matchbox-sized buildings on a tray. Keep it safe and add other details during future worships or family times.
* Draw your heavenly city plan like an illustrated map. Draw pictures showing where the different buildings and places would be and what they might look like.
* Research the different stones in the foundations of the New Jerusalem and draw a picture of what it might look like from the outside.

Bible Newspaper

Create a Bible newspaper.

Bible connection:

The apostle Paul wrote letters to many churches. He included all kinds of useful teaching, information, greetings, inspiration, prayers, and even some poetry, such as 1 Corinthians 13. When he wrote to Timothy, he also included health and lifestyle tips.

THINGS YOU NEED:

- Large sheets of paper, folded and stapled to make a small newspaper
- Extra paper
- Pens, pencils, erasers, marker pens, rulers, glue, scissors, etc.
- Some family-appropriate newspapers

Worship activities:

1. Look briefly at the newspapers you've collected. Which sections of the newspaper would you like to include in your Bible newspaper to make it positive, interesting, inspiring, and practical?
2. You could include Bible news stories as if they are just happening, features on biblical wisdom, a travel feature, Bible recipes, a Bible family-problem page, Bible cartoons, a Bible puzzle page, etc.
3. Decide who will write or create the various sections of your Bible newspaper, depending on each person's skills and interests. Make all enjoy their part of the project. Encourage your children to research their stories and features using your Bible study aids and the Internet.
4. You might want to work on the newspaper project for several worships.
5. Enjoy reading what each person has contributed. Do the puzzles together and talk about what you learned, or what you enjoyed the most, while doing this project.

Prayer:

- Imagine you are publishing a good news page about your family. What good news would you include in it this week? Tell each other your good news stories. Thank God for His blessings and for the good news of Jesus, who is the best news ever!

Other ideas:

- Use your computer to turn your creation into a printable newspaper. Share it with friends, relatives, and local church members. Send one to a missionary family or an isolated person.
- Choose a theme, such as Jesus' birth, and make a special newspaper to send instead of Christmas cards.
- Make a newspaper based on your own family faith stories, favorite recipes, hobbies, travel experiences, etc. to send as your annual newsletter.

Poetic Stories

Poetry has often been used as a way to make stories more memorable so they can be retained and passed on to future generations. Poems can also be set to music and become ballads and songs.

Bible connection:

Psalm 119. You don't have to read the entire psalm! Just show your children how every section of the psalm starts with a different letter of the alphabet.

THINGS YOU NEED:

- Paper, pencils, and erasers
- Examples of different kinds of poetry and how they are constructed—rhyming poems, free verse that doesn't rhyme, haiku, limericks, sonnets, etc.
- An example of a good Bible story in rhyme, or read Psalm 23 and compare it with other poems, hymns, and songs that have been based on the psalm.

Worship activities:

1. Read one of your favorite poetic psalms, or choose a favorite Bible story to inspire your poetic creativity.
2. Work together as a family to create a poem or write individual poems.
3. Perform or read your poems to each other.
4. Work on your poems, and perfect them, until they are ready to be printed in your church bulletin or newsletter.
5. You can also memorize the poems and present them in church during a special program.

Prayer:

- Write a rhyming prayer. First think of examples of rhyming prayers that you already know, such as a grace before meals. Or rewrite the Lord's Prayer as a poem.
- Let each person write a rhyming prayer of praise, thanks, confession, or prayer requests.
- Take turns choosing something to thank God for, and then let everyone else think of something to thank God for that rhymes with the first item.

Other ideas:

- If you have someone in the family who enjoys drawing, create a small rhyming storybook, illustrated with his or her pictures. Perhaps you could make such a book into a gift for a younger child in the family.
- Choose a psalm and rewrite the verses in rhyme. Keep a familiar tune in your mind as you work, and fit your words to the music, so that it can become a song.

Bible Verse Scrapbook

Make a collection of your family's favorite Bible verses, and illustrate them in creative and beautiful ways.

Bible connection:

"A word fitly spoken is like apples of gold in pictures of silver" (Proverbs 25:11, KJV). God's words are well-spoken, and we can make them even more beautiful by creating attractive settings for them.

THINGS YOU NEED:

- Promise box or a list of favorite Bible verses or memory verses
- A scrapbook or a binder filled with clear plastic pockets
- Various scrap papers and craft supplies
- Scissors, pens, ruler, adhesive, adhesive foam pads
- Decorative letters and stickers
- Plain paper, computer, and printer (optional)
- Books of scrapbooking designs from the library or scrapbooking Web sites to give you inspiration, ideas, and techniques

Worship activities:

1. Share your favorite Bible verses, or choose some verses from a promise box.
2. Ask everyone to choose a Bible verse and use the craft supplies to illustrate and decorate the verse in any way they like.
3. It may be helpful to print the chosen Bible verses using a computer, selecting appropriate and interesting fonts, and resizing the letters to suit the size of the scrapbook pages.
4. Help each other with ideas and techniques.
5. Insert your finished designs into your scrapbook or binder pockets.
6. Add new verses during future family worships.
7. This activity helps you to memorize the verses you are decorating.

Prayer:

- Decorate the Bible verses you have chosen and use them to inspire your prayers. Praise God for the wonderful verses in the Bible, claim the promises in the verses, or adapt the verses into prayers that apply to your own lives.

Other ideas:

- Instead of creating scrapbooking pages, turn your decorated verses into greeting cards or frame them to make inspiring wall art.
- Decorate verses about thankfulness, keeping the designs flat. Laminate them to make placemats for everyday use or for special occasions, such as Thanksgiving.
- Make miniature decorated verses that can be inserted into key fobs, badges, or small laminating wallets.
- Make simple bookmarks with Bible verses and flat collage materials to give as gifts.

Storylines

A storyline is a simple way of illustrating a story while it's being told. It doesn't need any particular talent because the pictures can be very simple.

Bible connection:

You can use any Bible story or passage you like, as long as it lends itself to drawing some simple shapes and patterns.

THINGS YOU NEED:

- Long strips of paper, such as drawing paper rolls, or the plain side of a roll of wallpaper cut into strips that are 6 inches (15 cm) wide, by as long as you want/need
- New, smooth-flowing marker pens
- Pencils, erasers, scissors

Worship activities:

1. Explain how to make a storyline. One person will read the Bible story from the Bible or a storybook. Everyone else will have a long roll of paper and a marker pen or pencil. As the person tells the story, everyone else draws one continuous line, illustrating the story with simple shapes, and trying not to take their pens off the paper. It's OK to take the pen off the paper if you need to move your body, but you must put the pen back on the paper where you left off.
2. So the story of Zacchaeus might include a line drawing of Jesus; the city of Jericho; Zacchaeus, a short man; a bag of money or coins; a crowd; a tree; Zacchaeus in a tree, etc. If possible, show an example of a storyline.
3. Give everyone the materials and space they need, and then tell the story, quite slowly. Pause after each verse to give everyone time to draw and keep up with you, so they don't feel too rushed.
4. When you have finished your story, look at the various storylines.
5. Invite a younger child to retell the story using his or her storyline.
6. Ask, "What did you like best about the story? What was the most important message in the story for you? What does this story help you to learn about God's love?"

Prayer:

- Draw storyline prayers. Say, "Dear Father, we praise You for . . . ; we thank you for . . . ; we're sorry for . . . ; and please can You help us with. . . . In Jesus' Name, Amen." In the pauses between the phrases, invite everyone to make a single line drawing of something that illustrates that part of the prayer for them.
- Share your storyline prayers, or let each person roll them up and keep them as private prayers.

Other ideas:

- Write the story in your own words, under the storyline you have drawn.
- If you have a video camera, try making a very simple film. Invite your child to tell the story in their own words as you slowly film along their storyline.

48

Story Plates

Have family worship during a special meal. Invite everyone to make their own food to illustrate their favorite Bible story.

Bible connection:

"Taste and see that the LORD is good!" (Psalm 34:8, NIV). This activity is a creative way to taste and see a Bible story and to experience God's goodness.

THINGS YOU NEED:

- A variety of your family's favorite foods, such as spreads, dips, crackers, cheese, cottage cheese, freshly washed fruit and vegetables, nuts, dried fruit, slices of bread, etc.
- Large plates or platters, or clean trays
- Safe knives
- Cookie-cutters in different shapes (optional)
- Toothpicks to connect 3-D shapes (optional)
- Heart-shaped desserts (optional)

Worship activities:

- Bring everyone to the table for worship and make sure everyone has clean hands.
- Read the Bible verse and bless the food.
- Invite each person to make the Bible-story scene using the food on the table. You may need to help younger children to cut and shape their food.
- Enjoy working together and being creative in any way you like.
- When everyone has finished, try to guess which story each story plate represents. Invite each plate's artist to talk about the picture and tell how it illustrates God's love and goodness.
- Then enjoy eating your pictures—and the rest of your meal.
- If you're serving a heart-shaped dessert, tell each other about a time you experienced God's love during the past week.

Prayer:

- Say another prayer at the end of your meal, taking turns thanking God for your favorite foods.

Other ideas:

- Take turns choosing a different food on the table and saying, "This food reminds me of God's love because it looks so beautiful, it strengthens me, it's sweet, He cares enough to make delicious food for us," etc.
- Help your children to design placemats that you can laminate and reuse. Write a variety of questions on them, asking your family: How did you experience God's love today? What filled you with wonder today? What did God help you to do well today? What ten things do you want to thank God for today? etc. Use them at the dinner table to help your family have faith-filled conversations.

Book Makers

Make interesting books of your favorite Bible stories.

Bible connection:

The Bible is really a library of books. It contains history books, law books, poetry, prophecy, stories, and letters.

THINGS YOU NEED:

- Paper
- Pens, coloring materials, scissors, adhesive, double-sided sticky tape
- Cardstock
- Scraps of interesting paper
- Envelopes
- Pictures from Bible coloring books
- Books from the library about making simple books, or ideas and information from the Internet
- Samples of miniature books, lift-the-flap books, pop-up books, etc.

Worship activities:

1. Choose a favorite Bible story.
2. Read the story from the Bible or a storybook.
3. Look at the samples of different books you have found and discuss how you could design, write, illustrate, and produce a simple storybook of the Bible story you have just read.
4. Work together to plan and design the book to see which words and pictures will fit best on each page.
5. Have fun helping your children to make the book special. Perhaps you will cut the pages into interesting shapes, or perhaps create pop-ups, add flaps, or tuck surprises into pockets and envelopes, etc.
6. If your children enjoy this kind of project, make more books in the future and learn more about creative book-making techniques.
7. Take the book to read to a younger child or to show to an elderly person when you visit him or her.

Prayer:

- Make a prayer scrapbook for your family. Include written prayers, prayer pictures and activities, lists and photos of people you're praying for, stories of answered prayers, and pictures of things you're thankful for, etc.

Other ideas:

- Instead of making a book, help your children to make an audio recording of a Bible story. Let them practice reading the story. Look for objects that will make suitable sound effects. Find music to accompany parts of the story. Record the story using your phone or computer and find a way to send the story to a grandparent or friend.
- If recording isn't possible, try using your phone or Skype®. Let your children read the story aloud and make the appropriate sound effects.

50

Wish You Were Here!

Create imaginary postcards from Bible characters to help you explore their stories and experiences.

Bible connection:

"I have much to write to you, but I do not want to use paper and ink. Instead, I hope to visit you and talk with you face to face, so that our joy may be complete" (2 John 12, NIV).

THINGS YOU NEED:

- Sample postcards that have been sent to your family
- Blank postcards or rectangles of white cardstock
- Coloring materials, scissors, adhesive, pencils, rulers, etc.
- Craft supplies and scraps
- Travel and holiday brochures, especially of Mediterranean-type areas
- A list of interesting Bible postcard possibilities:
  - A postcard from Noah during his "cruise" on the ark
  - A postcard from Mary and Joseph to their families, announcing the birth of Jesus, or while they are living in Egypt
  - A postcard from Jonah inside the whale or from Ninevah
  - A postcard from Joseph in Egypt to his brother Benjamin, at any time during his life there
  - A postcard from Ruth to her family back in Moab

Worship activities:

1. Show your family the postcards you've received. Pray for the people who sent them to you.
2. Read one of the Bible stories listed above. Imagine what the characters might have written if they could have sent a postcard to a friend or relative.
3. Then let everyone choose a Bible character and imagine what the character they chose would have written on a postcard, if they could have sent one.
4. Invite them to be as creative as they like, both in what they write and how they decorate or design their postcards, stamps, and postmarks.
5. Encourage them to think what the characters might enjoy most or least about where they are, and what they might want to say to their families, etc.
6. Give everyone time to complete and display their postcards.
7. What fresh ideas have you had about these Bible characters through doing this activity?

Prayer:

- Write and decorate postcards to God, praising Him, thanking Him, asking for forgiveness, and asking Him to help you and other people.

Another idea:

- What do you think God would love to write on a postcard to you? Create an imaginary postcard from God to you in which He tells you how wonderful heaven is and how much He longs for you to be with Him.

Family-Building Worships

OUR "COMFORT MENU"

INVENT A MACHINE

LOVE WAS HERE

SUPPORTING COLUMNS

FAMILY FAITH TREE

SPIRITUAL MILESTONES

VALUES TOWER

THE "INCREDIBLES"

HAPPY FAMILIES

FAMILY MEMORY BAG

51

Our "Comfort Menu"

Work together to create a list of different ways your family members like to be comforted when they are sad or distressed.

Bible connection:

"Praise be to the God and Father of our Lord Jesus Christ, the Father of compassion and the God of all comfort, who comforts us in all our troubles, so that we can comfort those in any trouble with the comfort we ourselves receive from God" (2 Corinthians 1:3, 4, NIV). Our loving Father wants to comfort us so we can comfort each other when life is sad and challenging.

THINGS YOU NEED:

- Paper
- Ballpoint pens
- Strong facial tissues

Worship activities:

1. Read the Bible verses and talk about God as our Comforter. How does God comfort us? What Bible verses do you find most comforting? Jesus came "to bind up the brokenhearted." What does that mean and how did Jesus comfort people? How has God comforted you in the past?
2. List at least 12 different ways in which the people in your family like to be comforted: a hug, having someone to listen to them, a mug of hot chocolate, going for a walk, a back rub, doing something fun together, etc.
3. Write out your list neatly, or print it using your computer. The list you have made together is your family's special "Comfort Menu."
4. Whenever anyone feels sad, ill, or upset, encourage them to either choose something from the menu of comforting options or add a new idea to the list.
5. When do you think each person in your family most needs to be comforted? How can you make sure that you're comforting them in the best way possible?
6. When we comfort each other, we show each other God's loving comfort. When we don't know how to comfort each other, God can show us how.

Prayer:

- Pray for the people you know who need some comfort. Write their names on a facial tissue using a ballpoint pen. Ask God to comfort them, and ask Him to show you how you can be their comforters too.
- Now do something practical to comfort the people you have prayed for—make a card, plan a visit, give them a call, hug them, etc.

Another idea:

- Role-play each person in your family feeling sad and then choosing something from the "Comfort Menu." Take turns being the comforter and comforting the sad person in the way they like best.

Invent a Machine

Every family faces challenges and stress points. Invent the machine your family (and probably many others) would love to own.

Bible connection:

"Live in harmony with one another" (Romans 12:16, NIV). When we live in harmony with each other and cooperate together, everyone is happier.

THINGS YOU NEED:

- Large sheets of plain white paper
- Pencils and erasers
- Marker pens or crayons

Worship activities:

1. Read the Bible verse. Talk about a time when your family experienced harmony and everyone was happy, kind, and helping each other. What helped you to get along so well?
2. Then talk about the times when you often find it difficult to work together harmoniously, such as getting ready in the morning or struggles over meals. Don't blame anyone; talk about it as a problem the whole family shares.
3. Think about the families in the Bible who had problems getting along at times, such as Jacob and Esau, or Jacob's sons. Even great families have their challenges!
4. Imagine that your family could buy or make a machine that would help you manage the less harmonious times. What would it be?
5. Work together as a family to design an imaginary machine that your family really needs. Maybe you need a lunch-packing machine, a helping-children-go-to-sleep machine, or a finding-lost-things machine.
6. Talk about how the machine might work. Scribble and draw your ideas around the edges of a large piece of paper.
7. Then bring your best ideas together to design your unique machine.
8. What will you call your special invention? What difference would this machine make to your family and to each one of you?
9. Because you can't really have this machine, what could each of you do to help solve the challenge so that you can live together in harmony? Help each other, plan ahead, be kind, don't complain, create a different routine, etc.

Prayer:

- Pray about a special challenge your family is facing.
- Ask God to help each one of you lovingly play your part so that you can live in harmony like a well-designed machine.

Other ideas:

- Build your imaginary machine out of your children's construction toys.
- Or use boxes and junk to build your machine. Include elastic bands, paper fasteners, string, and paper clips to create a moving model.

53

Love Was Here

Every time we do something kind and loving for each other, we feel closer together, happier, and more loved. We also experience more of God's love through the love we share with each other.

Bible connection:

"I have loved you with an everlasting love; I have drawn you with unfailing kindness" (Jeremiah 31:3, NIV). God's love inspires every loving action we do. How can we show each other His love by doing kind things for each other?

THINGS YOU NEED:

- Plain paper in a variety of colors
- Pencils, erasers, and scissors
- Marker pens

Worship activities:

1. Fold each sheet of colored paper twice so it is four sheets thick. Make a heart-shaped template, draw around it on the top of the folded sheet, and cut four hearts at once. Repeat to make a stack of hearts.
2. Talk about the times when someone did something very kind and loving for you. What was it and how did it make you feel? How do you feel when you do something loving for someone else? What are the three most loving things that the people in your family could do for you?
3. Divide the hearts among the family members and write the words "Love was here" on each one.
4. Decorate the heart shapes using marker pens.
5. Give each person a few hearts and put the rest in a basket.
6. Discuss what Jesus would do to show His love if He came into your home today and did some kind things.
7. Ask everyone to do loving things for each other and to leave a love heart close to the place where they did the loving thing, such as under a glass of water, on the pillow of a tidied bed, in the pocket of a freshly laundered pair of jeans, or in a lunch box.

Prayer:

- Make a list of all the things God has done to show His love for each of you. Thank Him for His loving kindness.
- Make a list of things you could each do to show love to each other. Pray that God will help you to do these loving things for each other.

Other ideas:

- Use wooden clothes pins instead of paper notes. Write the words "Love was here" on them and clip them to the places where a loving action has taken place.
- Decorate your hearts with stickers to make them extra special.
- Encourage everyone to do one kind act for someone else every day.

Supporting Columns

When we're working toward a goal, we need people to support us, in the way that a column supports a statue like Nelson's Column in London or the Columbus Monument in Barcelona.

Bible connection:

"Encourage one another and build each other up" (1 Thessalonians 5:11, NIV). Sometimes our goals are very big, or they take a long time to achieve. God gives us loving families to support us with their encouragement.

THINGS YOU NEED:

- Sheets of strong paper or lightweight cardstock
- Marker pens, scissors, adhesive tape, double-sided tape, or glue sticks
- A copy of a photograph of each person

Worship activities:

1. Talk about the various ways Jesus supported and encouraged His friends, disciples, and the people He met who were struggling.
2. Read the Bible verse and ask everyone how they most like to be encouraged and where they need extra encouragement at the moment.
3. Think about the people in the Bible who encouraged and supported others: Aaron supported Moses; Ruth supported Naomi; Mordecai supported Esther; Jonathan supported David; Dorcas supported widows, etc.
4. Ask each person to think of a special goal they would like to achieve, such as passing a test, learning a new skill, or working on a character strength.
5. Give each person a sheet of paper or cardstock. Ask them to write one of their goals clearly at the top (narrow side) of their piece of paper, leaving the top 2 inches (4 cm) free, and leaving 2 inches (4 cm) on each side.
6. Cut out a picture of each person. Glue the bottom of the picture onto the top of the piece of paper, just above their goals.
7. Pass the papers around the circle and write simple prayers, promises of support, or encouraging messages on each person's sheet. Younger children can draw pictures.
8. When everyone has finished, return the sheets to their owners, so they can read the messages and be encouraged.
9. Curve each piece of paper into a tall cylinder and stick the two long edges together to make a column. The photo should stand up above the column to make a statue. If it flops over, add extra support behind the figure.
10. Keep the columns in places where they will continue to be encouraging.
11. Follow through on your promises to support each other.

Prayer:

- Pray an encouraging prayer for the person on your left.

Other ideas:

- Fasten your papers around sturdy round cookie or chip cartons to turn your columns

into pencil pots.
- Whenever a goal has been reached, celebrate by sticking a gold star onto your column to show when a goal has been reached.

Family Faith Tree

Help your family explore their important spiritual heritage. Whatever your family believed, or didn't believe, there are important lessons to be learned.

Bible connection:

Psalm 78:1–8. Faith, beliefs, values, and character-building stories are passed from generation to generation, to strengthen families and inspire their faith in God.

THINGS YOU NEED:

- Large sheets of paper
- Pencils and erasers
- Sticky notes (optional)
- Marker pens

Worship activities:

1. Draw your family tree. Sketch it lightly in pencil to make sure you have space for everyone. Then write in the names and relationships using the marker pens. You will need lots of space around each person's name.
2. Think about each person in turn. What do you think are their three most important beliefs and character strengths? Write them next to their name. If you run out of space, draw a line from their name to a place on the edge of the paper where there is more room.
3. A belief might relate to their faith, how they worshipped, or how they chose to live their lives. A character strength might be generosity, kindness, putting others first, making sacrifices for the benefit of their children, working hard, showing courage, etc.
4. What are the most important beliefs and character strengths of each person in your family? Write them under each of your names.
5. Then look at your family faith tree and talk about the questions below.
   - How did the beliefs and character strengths of your family members help them to live their lives well?
   - What effect did their beliefs have on their lives?
   - What effect did their lives have on their beliefs?
   - How has God been working in your family over the past few generations?

Prayer:

- Pray for each of the people or families that you have included on your family tree.
- Thank God for leading and guiding your family for generations.

Other ideas:

- Interview your Christian relatives about their faith journeys, beliefs, answered prayers, etc.
- Make a scrapbook of family photos and family faith stories to inspire your children.

56

Spiritual Milestones

In the Bible many great men celebrated the amazing things God did for them by building stone altars. Make your own collection of stones to remind your family of the amazing things God has done in your lives.

Bible connection:

Joshua 4:1–8. The twelve tribes of Israel built a stone altar to remind them, and the future generations of their children, how God helped them to cross the river Jordan to the Promised Land.

THINGS YOU NEED:

- Stones of different kinds, shapes, and sizes
- Permanent marker pens

Worship activities:

1. Talk about the spiritual milestones in your family. Perhaps the milestones might be answers to prayers, choosing to follow God, a baptism, the birth of a baby, miracles, being involved in helping others, or moments of total wonder.
2. As you talk about each milestone, invite someone to choose a stone that particularly symbolizes the moment or the memory. A big event might be illustrated with a larger stone. One that sparkles might remind you of a wedding or other happy event. A rough stone might represent a time when God helped you through a difficult experience. A white stone might remind you of a wedding or baptism.
3. When you have finished talking about your milestones, arrange the stones in a design. Lay them out in a flat pattern, stack them in a pile, or place them in a large, simple vase.
4. Add other stones, in the future, to mark the special events in your lives.

Prayer:

- Hold hands around the stones you have chosen. Thank God for guiding and protecting your family.
- Or use permanent marker pens to write sentence prayers on some of the larger stones and arrange them as a display in your garden.

Other ideas:

- Create a stone sculpture by sticking your stones onto a stable base using extra-strong adhesive.
- Use permanent marker pens to write a word or two on each stone, to remind you of the wonderful things that God has done for you and your family.
- Use objects, twigs, or shells, etc., instead of stones.

Values Tower

As Christian parents we want to pass on our important values to our children. Here's a way of exploring your family values together.

Bible connection:

"He has shown you, O mortal, what is good. And what does the LORD require of you? To act justly and to love mercy and to walk humbly with your God" (Micah 6:8, NIV). This is a summary of the important values God wants us to live by. What other values are important to you as a Christian family?

THINGS YOU NEED:

- 25 large plain index cards or sheets of paper cut in half
- Marker pens
- Reusable adhesive (such as Sticky Tack®) for sticking the index cards to a wall or door, so you can move them around during the activity

Worship activities:

1. Read the Bible verse and explain the various values it contains. Ask family members to think of other values that are important guides for our lives, such as honesty, kindness, sharing, showing respect, being patient, putting others first, forgiving each other, being loving, taking care of the earth, worshiping God, and keeping each other safe. When have you seen each other living by good values recently?
2. As the various values are mentioned, write them on separate index cards or sheets of paper. Write at least 10 to 12.
3. Think about each of the values and decide which are the most important ones for your family.
4. Work together to make a tower of value cards, by using reusable adhesive to attach them to a safe surface, such as a door. Leave plenty of space between each card so you can add other cards and move the value cards around. Put your most important values at the top of the tower.
5. Talk about each of the values as you work. How do you live them out? Why might one be more important than another? Or would you rather arrange the cards in a different way to show that some are equally important?

Prayer:

- Pray that God will help each of you to live according to His important values. Pray about some of the challenges you face as a family as you try to live out your values in a complicated and broken world.

Other ideas:

- Encourage older children to find a Bible verse about each of the values you have chosen.
- Make a poster of your top ten family values. Write them out in a simple and appealing way and print a copy from your computer. Frame them and hang them where they'll be seen every day.

58

The "Incredibles"

This fun family worship activity helps you to discover the spiritually gifted people in your family! It's very important to nurture your children's spiritual gifts and to encourage them to use them. The more they use their gifts, the more gifts will be added to their lives.

Bible connection:

1 Corinthians 12:4–11 and Romans 12:6–8. God gives each one of us special gifts so that we can help each other, work together, and be stronger than when we are alone.

THINGS YOU NEED:

- A loaf of bread, a jar of peanut butter, a jar of jelly or jam, a table knife, and a plate. Wrap each item like a gift. (Add more items if you have a larger family, or wrap two together if you have a smaller family, varying the ingredients to suit your family.)
- Marker pens
- Plastic name badges and insert cards (choose ones you can color easily).

Worship activities:

1. The Holy Spirit gives everyone who follows Jesus some special gifts for them to enjoy using so they can bless other people.
2. Give each person one of the gifts you have wrapped, and let everyone open their gifts. Let them work out what to do with their strange collection of presents! They are all good gifts, but not so useful on their own. Point out that when everyone shares their gifts, then everyone can enjoy a sandwich.
3. Think about each person in your family and analyze their spiritual gifts. What kind of spiritual "super gifts" have they been given? How does the Holy Spirit help them use their spiritual "super gifts" to help your family and other people?
4. Who has the super gift of comforter, fixer, tidier, smiler, gardener, brave person, peace-maker, etc. in your family?
5. Create some spiritual super-gift badges for each of you to wear, with pictures of your own "super gifts."
6. Talk about the times your family most needs each of your children's super gifts. Discuss how they could use them. Explain that the Holy Spirit's gifts are to be used and shared so that they can help everyone.

Prayer:

- Pray for each person in your family, thanking God for giving them their spiritual gifts, blessing them, and praying that the Holy Spirit will show them how to use their gifts to share God's love.

Other ideas:

- Think of some ways in which each of you can use your special spiritual gifts to help other people understand more about God's love.
- Create a fun way of announcing that a spiritual gift is needed, so that a "gifted" person can come running to the rescue.

Happy Families

What makes a happy family? What does the Bible say about how to have happy families and good relationships? Happy Christian families are amazing examples of God's love in action. How can you add a little extra happiness to your home?

Bible connection:

"Unless the LORD builds the house, the builders labor in vain" (Psalm 127:1, NIV). We need to build our families according to God's plans for us, because He wants our relationships to be the best they can be.

THINGS YOU NEED:

- One or two large appliance-type boxes, with no writing on the outside
- Lining wallpaper and glue (optional, to cover the box if necessary)
- Thick marker pens, large sticky notes (or plain paper and glue sticks)

Worship activities:

1. Work together to create a simple house from the boxes.
2. Make the outside walls as plain as possible, perhaps by opening up the boxes and reconstructing them inside out, or by covering the "house" with paper.
3. Read what the Bible says about good family relationships (Romans 12; 1 Corinthians 13; Ephesians 5:21–33, etc.). Then talk about what makes your family a happy place to live.
4. Write your ideas on the sticky notes and stick them onto the walls of the house. Leave the roof free. You'll write prayers on it later.
5. Ask younger children to draw pictures of the things they like about your family. Stick their pictures onto the house.
6. When you have all finished writing and drawing, look around the house together and read all your ideas. Ask the children to tell you about their pictures.
7. Then ask, "What do we do that makes our home happy? When do you feel happiest?"
8. Invite each person to suggest one thing they could do to make your family even happier.
9. God has given us good information about how to have happy families because He knows how important it is for us to feel loved, happy, and safe. We learn most about His love from the love, forgiveness, help, and acceptance we experience in our families.

Prayer:

- Invite each person to write a short prayer for your family on the roof of the house you have made. Join hands in a circle and pray for your family.

Another idea:

- Draw the outline of a large house on a large plain sheet of card or paper. Write your ideas inside the outline or on sticky notes that can be stuck to the house picture.

60

Family Memory Bag

Make a memory bag filled with small objects to help you remember your important family events.

Bible connection:

"Behind the second curtain was a room called the Most Holy Place, which had the golden altar of incense and the gold-covered ark of the covenant. This ark contained the gold jar of manna, Aaron's staff that had budded, and the stone tablets of the covenant" (Hebrews 9:3, 4, NIV). When Moses and his craftsmen created the Ark of the Covenant for the ancient tabernacle, they put several very special objects into the box to remind them how miraculously God had protected and cared for them.

THINGS YOU NEED:

- A small cloth bag with a drawstring closure to use as a memory bag
- Lots of small objects that will remind your family members of different things that have happened to them such as stones, foreign coins, shells, toy cars, adhesive bandages, birthday candles, and plastic animals (If you aren't sure what to put in your bag, or are short of time, send your family on an object hunt. Ask each person to find three or four objects that remind them of things that have happened in your family.)
- An alarm or timer you can set for one minute

Worship activities:

1. Show your family the memory bag and explain that there are lots of different objects in the bag that might remind them of a variety of events that have happened in your family.
2. Pass the bag around the circle. Each person picks an unseen object from the bag and has one minute (use an alarm or timer) to tell a family story that somehow involves their object.
3. Their object is returned to the bag, and the bag is passed to the next person. No one is allowed to tell the same story twice. If an object is chosen twice, a different story must be told or a new object chosen.
4. Why do you think God wanted the children of Israel to keep a box of special reminders with them as they traveled through the wilderness?
5. What treasures and reminders do you think God would want you to carry in your memory bag to remind you of His love and protection?

Prayer:

- Take turns choosing an object from the bag. Thank God for the happy events in your lives and for the blessing of happy memories.

Other ideas:

- Use the memory bag activity in the car or at special family dinners.
- Find little objects at yard sales and thrift stores to add to your story bag so that there are a variety of things to be found and new stories to be told.
- If it's hard to find the objects you want, stick pictures onto index cards and add them to your bag.

Worships Based on Parables

LITTLE THINGS MAKE A BIG DIFFERENCE

THE BEST PARTY EVER!

WHO IS MY NEIGHBOR?

THE TWO HOUSES

KEEP ON PRAYING!

THE MEN WHO SOLD EVERYTHING

LOST AND FOUND!

BIGGER BARNS?

GIFTED

SALTY

61

Little Things Make a Big Difference

In God's kingdom a widow's penny is as valuable as a rich man's bag of gold; a tiny seed grows into a huge tree; and a small amount of yeast can transform a whole batch of bread.

Bible connection:

"He told them another parable: 'The kingdom of heaven is like a mustard seed, which a man took and planted in his field. Though it is the smallest of all seeds, yet when it grows, it is the largest of garden plants and becomes a tree, so that the birds come and perch in its branches' " (Matthew 13:31, 32, NIV).

THINGS YOU NEED:

- A collection of small things that can make a big difference, e.g., penny, eraser, pencil, seed, battery, key, button, match, salt, postage stamp
- A bag to hide and contain all the small things

Worship activities:

1. Read the short parable of the mustard seed. Ask your family what they think the parable really means.
2. Pass the bag around. Take a tiny item out of the bag and say how this tiny object could make a huge difference. (If you are missing a penny, you may not be able to buy what you want. A pencil can write a book that can change the world. A battery can make something work. A match can start a fire that can burn down a forest, etc.)
3. Jesus said that even if we have only a small amount of faith, it will make a huge difference to our lives. Once we start to believe in Jesus, He can transform our lives and make miracles happen.
4. What about your children? Even though they are small or young, they can still make a big difference. They can choose to help, smile, say kind things, share, encourage others, pray for others, tell their friends about Jesus, etc.

Prayer:

- Think about some tiny things you do to share God's love. Pray that God will use the little things you do to make a big difference to someone else's life.

Other ideas:

- Use yeast to make bread with your children. Show them how a small amount of yeast can double the size of the dough.
- Throw tiny stones into a pool or lake and watch the ripples expand over a wide distance.
- Plant a small fruit tree with your children so that in many years' time there'll be a fruit-bearing tree for others to enjoy.

The Best Party Ever!

God is planning the best party ever! Let's make sure we don't miss it!

Bible connection:
The parable of the great banquet. Luke 14:15–24.

THINGS YOU NEED:

* Paper and pens
* (Optional) Party invitations written from God to each person in your family: Venue—heaven; Date and time—when Jesus comes again; Add "Come as you are because I love you! Your Father God."

Worship activities:
1. Read the parable of the great banquet.
2. Imagine your family is helping a king to plan the best party ever!
3. What would you include on the menu? What would you drink? What entertainment and games would there be? What theme would you choose? What would you like people to wear? How would you decorate the room or garden, etc.? Be as creative as you like because kings have lots of money, and they like to have very special parties.
4. Write down all your ideas and encourage your children to be excited about them.
5. Then imagine that everything is ready for the wonderful party, but everyone who has been invited has sent their excuses. Read the excuses in the story again and suggest what kinds of excuses people might make today. I've just bought a new car and I need to take it for a drive; I'm trying to complete my latest computer game; I'm too busy shopping during the sales; I'm working overtime, etc.
6. Ask how you and your family can make sure that you're ready for the best party ever. How can you be like the servants and invite other people to God's party?
7. Give everyone an invitation from God to the best party ever, in heaven. It's the party that will never end! What answer will each person give to God?

Prayer:
* Hold hands around your invitations. Thank God that He is planning the best party ever. Pray that you'll be ready for the party when Jesus comes again.
* Pray about the people you want to bring to Jesus. Pray that they will stop making excuses and choose to follow Him.

Other ideas:
* End your worship with a small party celebration, even if it's just a special juice drink in a fancy glass.
* Give your children a small party bag with a few tiny Christian treats in it.

— 63 —

Who Is My Neighbor?

The Good Samaritan is one of Jesus' most famous parables. How can we care for others too?

Bible connection:

Luke 10:25–37, the parable of the good Samaritan. The Samaritan does everything he can to help a stranger. How can we help those around us?

THINGS YOU NEED:

- Paper and crayons or markers
- Scissors
- Rough cloth or a beige towel to make a desert
- Twine or a strip of fabric to mark the road
- Scraps of fabric or paper to scrunch and make "rocks"
- A small box for an inn, and a larger box for Jerusalem
- First-aid supplies
- Leaflets about caring organizations in your community

Worship activities:

1. Read the Bible story. Invite each person to draw and color some of the following people: the walking traveler, the injured traveler, the robbers, the priest, the Levite, the good Samaritan and his donkey, and the innkeeper. Or find images on the Internet that you can print and color.
2. Cut out the shapes so each person is separate and can be moved around.
3. Lay out the desert and the road, with the inn at one end and Jerusalem at the other end. Hide the robbers behind the "rocks." Then let the children retell the story, using the characters you have made. Let them use their imagination to retell the story in their own way.
4. After the story, ask them who are the neighbors of the priest, the Levite, the Samaritan, the innkeeper, and finally the robbers. In fact, we are all neighbors to each other, especially when people are in need.
5. Ask your children what they could do to help someone who had been hurt. They can't take them to an inn, but they could run for help, call an ambulance, offer some water, etc.
6. Think about your "neighbors" in your community—those who really need your help. Look at the information leaflets about the caring organizations in your city. Find out what they do and how you can help. Choose a practical way to support one of them and involve your children in the activity.

Prayer:

- Pray for the people in your community who are lonely and struggling. Pray for the organizations that are caring for them.

Other ideas:

- Make a care package for a special need in your community.
- Teach your children how to call the emergency services, how to explain clearly where they are and what has happened, and how to do simple first aid.

The Two Houses

Jesus told this story to help us build our lives on the best principles—His love and His commandments.

Bible connection:
Matthew 7:24–27. Building our lives without good foundations is a waste of time!

THINGS YOU NEED:

- 2 sheets of clear acetate
- A water-soluble marker pen that will write on the acetate
- A permanent marker pen that will write on the acetate
- A bowl with a flat base
- A pitcher of water
- A large, smooth rock

Worship activities:
1. Ask your children to draw a large house on each sheet of acetate. Draw the house with the water-soluble pen on one sheet, and with the permanent pen on the other sheet.
2. The house drawn with the water-soluble pen represents the house built on the sand. The one drawn with the permanent pen represents the house built on the rock.
3. Stand the pictures of the two houses in the bowl.
4. Now read or tell the Bible story. When you read about the storm, let your children pour lots of water slowly over the two houses. One house will disappear, or at least smudge, but the permanent house will stay.
5. Hold the large rock. Think about the important and lasting principles on which Jesus wants us to build our lives, such as His love and forgiveness, generosity, humility, kindness, and honesty.
6. Write these principles on the rock as a reminder to build your lives on Jesus, and not on things that don't last.

Prayer:
- Ask Jesus to help you build your lives on Him. Pray that He will help you to live by the principles you wrote on the rock.
- Draw an outline of a house and write a prayer for your home inside the shape.

Another idea:
- Use wooden bricks. Fill one bowl with sand and build a house on the sand. Place a large rock or flat paver in a second bowl, and then add sand around the edges. Build a house on this "rock." Carefully pour water into the sand around the edges of each bowl so that the sand-based house crashes down, but the rock-based house stands firm.

Keep on Praying!

The story of the persistent widow reminds us that God wants us to keep praying and not give up, even when God doesn't answer right away.

Bible connection:

Luke 18:1–8. A poor widow needs help. She doesn't stop asking for help until she gets what she is owed. But God wants to help us far more willingly than the corrupt judge wanted to help the widow.

THINGS YOU NEED:

- Ingredients for a simple treat, such as a favorite sandwich, a fruit salad, or smoothie. Keep them in a bag in another room
- A recipe or instructions for making the treat
- A printout of a simple calendar or a purchased calendar

Worship activities:

1. Read the Bible story and talk about how we are like, or not like, the widow in the story. Also discuss how the judge is like, or not like, God.
2. Tell your family that you want to give them a special treat of whatever food you have prepared.
3. Leave one parent/adult in charge of the activity and have the other parent, another adult, or an older child leave the room to make a long phone call to a family member or friend. Make sure they take the bag of ingredients you need.
4. The adult with the children tries to help them make the treat, and everyone looks for the right ingredients, but they are nowhere to be found. Send a child to the other person to ask for what you need. Tell them to ask quietly and to keep on asking until they get what you need.
5. Let them ask at least three or four times before they are given an ingredient.
6. Each time they discover that they need another ingredient, send them, or another child, to ask again, in the same way. Keep doing this until you have all the things you need to make your treat. Then make and enjoy the treat.
7. Discuss how this experience illustrates our need to keep on praying. Emphasize that God delights to answer our prayers because He loves us.

Prayer:

- Print a simple calendar. Choose a prayer request that is very important to your family. Let your children draw a line through the date on the calendar every day your family prays for that request. Write on the calendar the Bible verse "Pray continually" (1 Thessalonians 5:17, NIV).

Another idea:

- Make a prayer jar. Decorate a label and write your special prayer request on it. Every time you pray for your prayer request, add a coin to the jar. Use the coins you collect to answer someone else's prayer. Through an aid organization such as ADRA, donate the money to buy vaccines, a chicken, or seeds for an overseas family.

The Men Who Sold Everything

These parables tell us that God's kingdom is so precious that we need to be willing to give up everything for it.

Bible connection:

Matthew 13:44–46. When we find the treasure of God's love, it's worth more than everything we have.

THINGS YOU NEED:

- A dollhouse, furniture, a toy car, etc.— toys that represent everything a merchant might own, or a toy farm or garage full of cars if you don't have a dollhouse
- A handful of small coins or buttons
- A Bible storybook that your children would enjoy
- A large "pearl" (circle cut from pearly or white paper), or small golden "coins" (smaller circles cut from yellow paper)

Worship activities:

1. Arrange the dollhouse to look like a home.
2. Read the Bible story together. Imagine a man finding something so precious that he is willing to become homeless to own it.
3. Show your children the book you have found for them. Say that you'll give it to them when they've earned enough money by selling you the furniture from the dollhouse. You may need to explain that this is a kind of story and you'll return all their toys at the end!
4. Invite your children to bring a few items at a time from the dollhouse to "sell" to you. Give them a coin or two in return. When they ask if the items are enough, shake your head and say "No, not yet. You'll need more money than that!"
5. Let them keep selling their toys to you until you have bought everything.
6. Then tell them that they have enough money to buy the book.
7. How is this activity like the story of the men who sold everything? What might it be like to "sell" everything? What's the most important message in this story?

Prayer:

- On the pearl or coins, list all the "treasures" that God has given you because you have chosen to follow Jesus: forgiveness, hope, the promise of heaven, a loving family, warm church fellowship, kindness and support, etc. Then thank God for all these treasures.

Another idea:

- What can your family give up to help others experience God's love? Collect some good quality things that your family no longer needs and give them to a charity-run resale store. Or sell them in a yard sale and use the money to buy gifts for needy children.

67

Lost and Found!

God loves each one of us so much that He's willing to do whatever it takes to find us and save us.

Bible connection:

Luke 15:3–7; Matthew 18:14, the parable of the lost sheep.

THINGS YOU NEED:

- White paper for cutting out many sheep shapes. Write the words of the Bible story from a modern translation on the sheep, writing one phrase, or a few words, on each shape. Leave out all the *sheep* words. Draw a sheep, or write the word *sheep* for as many times as the word *sheep* is mentioned in the story. Hide the sheep around the worship room.
- A special drink or meal for celebrating the return of the lost sheep
- Green fabric or paper, length of yarn, several toy sheep (or use the plain side of the sheep used in the worship activity), a toy or picture of a shepherd

Worship activities:

1. Read the Bible story and talk about the times when you or your children have been lost. How did you feel when you knew you were lost, or that you had lost each other? How did it feel to be found again?
2. Give your children the words of the Bible passage to arrange in the correct order. Soon they will realize that the "sheep" are missing.
3. Once they have finished arranging the rest of the words, send them on a hunt to find the lost "sheep."
4. When all the "sheep" have been found and placed in the right positions in the story, celebrate together. Pour everyone a delicious drink or enjoy a tasty "party" together.
5. Organize worship so that your celebration meal can follow worship at the time you usually eat. You could even make a sheep-shaped pizza or other sheep-themed food for a surprise.

Prayer:

- Lay a green cloth or paper on the floor to make a field or landscape. Use a piece of yarn to make a sheepfold. Thank God for finding you and saving you, and place your sheep in the fold. Pray for your friends and relatives who are still "wandering" and "lost," and place their sheep on the grass outside the fold. Pick up the shepherd and pray that God will look for the lost sheep, find them, and bring them into His fold.

Another idea:

- Make a lost sheep lift-the-flap book for young children. Use an old calendar with pictures of landscapes. Cut small flaps in suitable places on the landscapes, and cover the back of each flap with stiff white paper. Cut out a small picture of a sheep and place a small piece of reusable adhesive on the back of the sheep. Move the sheep so it can hide behind different flaps. Young children can search for the sheep as you tell them the story.

Bigger Barns?

Jesus told the story of a farmer who kept storing his grain in bigger barns. He was selfish because he didn't trust God to look after his needs in the future.

Bible connection:

Luke 12:13–21, 32–34, the parable of the rich fool. God gives us generous gifts to share with each other, not to hoard up selfishly for ourselves.

THINGS YOU NEED:

- A small container or a clean, empty jelly or jam jar for each person.
- A selection of larger jars and containers
- Tablespoon
- A large bag of popping corn; a large pan for popping corn; oil, butter, and salt for seasoning corn, etc.

Worship activities:

1. Give each person a jar. Put a tablespoon of popping corn into each jar.
2. Choose one person to be the rich farmer and fill their jar to overflowing with popping corn. Say, "I have even more corn for you here. What would you like me to do with it now this jar is full?" Maybe they will ask you to put the extra corn into another jar for them. Keep pouring and filling up jars of corn with their "harvest."
3. How do those with only a few kernels respond when one person is given so much? What does the "rich farmer" want to do with the big harvest of corn?
4. Maybe your children will notice that others have only a little corn and ask you to give some of the spare corn to them. If so, say, "That's a good idea!" and pour more corn into the other jars until everyone has the same amount. Or prompt them to share by asking, "What shall we do about those who don't have as much corn as you have?"
5. If the "rich farmer" keeps all his corn, suggest that those who only have a little corn might like to make popcorn with it for everyone to enjoy. Use only the corn from these "poor" farmers. Make it good and tasty.
6. Offer everyone the choice of the fresh popcorn or some unpopped corn. Everyone would much rather eat the delicious shared popcorn than the unpopped corn from the rich man's jar "barns."
7. Read the parable of the rich fool and ask how the popcorn-jar activity is like the story of the rich fool.
8. Make more popcorn together, using the corn from the "big barns" jar. Enjoy sharing it because everything tastes better when it's shared.

Prayer:

- Pray a popcorn prayer. This is a prayer when any person can say a sentence, or a word or two, at any time, like popping corn.

Another idea:

- Make bags of delicious popcorn to share with others. Give it away. Or sell it for a few pennies and raise funds to feed the hungry.

69

Gifted

Jesus told the parable of the talents to remind us that when we use our talents and gifts to bless others, He will give us even more!

Bible connection:

Matthew 25:14–29, the parable of the talents. "Each of you should use whatever gift you have received to serve others" (1 Peter 4:10, NIV). We need to discover and use the gifts God has given us.

THINGS YOU NEED:

- A gift bag for each child containing a few supplies to make something that will bless others. Choose activities that they will enjoy, and only give them a small amount of materials e.g., the supplies to make and decorate one greeting card or bookmark; the ingredients to make a small food gift; a kit to make a small sun-catcher, key fob or wooden project; a small plant to repot and give away
- Another gift bag for each child containing at least twice the amount of materials than they were originally given.
- Some large gift tags or greeting cards
- Pens

Worship activities:

1. Read the parable of the talents, or find an interesting narrative in a Bible storybook or video clip.
2. Talk about the various talents, gifts, and learned skills that each of you have and how they have been used to share God's love with others.
3. Give your children their first gift bag of supplies. Help them to use the gifts to make something that will bless other people. Make the experience as enjoyable as possible for your children.
4. When they have used everything in that bag, surprise them with a bigger gift bag, with even more supplies, to use in the future.
5. Talk about the story of the talents and why it's so important to use the gifts God gives us, so we can practice them, improve them, watch them grow, and find fresh and new ways to share God's love with others.

Prayer:

- Write each person's name on a separate greeting card. Pass the cards around and write things inside like "I thank God for your gift of . . . which I have seen you use to bless others when . . ." After everyone has written their thanks, give everyone their cards. Pray that God will help you use your gifts wisely and well.

Another idea:

- Start a small investment project. Give your children a small amount of money to buy the supplies to grow tomatoes, bake bread, make homemade lemonade, etc. Help them to sell their produce. Show them that their hard work has helped their money to grow. Reinvest the profits in another project, or give the money to a charity.

Salty

Jesus told His followers that they were like salt. What does that mean?

Bible connection:

"You are the salt of the earth" (Matthew 5:13, NIV). How can we be the salt of the earth?

THINGS YOU NEED:

- Several saltshakers filled with inexpensive salt, or a bowl of salt and spoons
- A small piece of food that tastes better with a little salt
- Several bowls and containers filled with water and frozen to make ice
- A large tray, plastic box, or bowl with sides deep enough to hold the melted water. (Cover your table with an old towel; this activity will be wet and messy!)
- Liquid watercolor paint or food coloring and plastic droppers
- White glue and black cardstock

Worship activities:

1. Read Matthew 5:13. Look at the saltshakers and discuss why Jesus called us the salt of the earth. In Jesus' time salt was so precious that Roman soldiers were paid with it, giving us the word *salary*.
2. Think of some other uses for salt, such as it makes food taste better and preserves it, it can be mixed with water and used to wash wounds to prevent infection, and it melts the ice on roads to prevent accidents. The information at http://www .saltinstitute.org says that there are over 14,000 known uses for salt.
3. Taste some food without salt. Then add a little salt to taste the difference.
4. Loosen the frozen ice. Lay the ice domes in the large bowl and let your children sprinkle a little salt over them. Watch the salt melt the ice into little gullies and rivulets. Then use droppers to drop different colors of paint or food coloring onto the ice. The colors highlight the patterns that the salt is making as it continues to melt through the ice.
5. Pick up a piece of melting, colored ice to see the patterns more clearly.
6. Discuss how this activity and the other good uses of salt help you to understand what it means to be the salt of the earth—melting hearts for Jesus, letting His colors of love show in the world, etc.

Prayer:

- Use the white glue to write the word *Jesus* on the black cardstock. Sprinkle the glue letters with salt and shake off any excess. Use the droppers to add small drops of food coloring or paint to the salt, and watch how the salt draws the colors along the letters. Let each person hold the saltshaker and pray that they will help others to experience Jesus.

Another idea:

- Serve unsalted soup. After letting your children taste the soup, add a little salt to show that it only takes a small amount to make a big difference to the flavor. Even though your children may only do small things to show God's love, it can make a big difference to the lives of the people around them.

SECTION 8

Worships Based on Special Bible Passages

GENESIS 1 AND 2—THE SEVEN GIFTS OF CREATION

PSALM 23—WALKING WITH THE SHEPHERD

PSALM 139—GOD KNOWS YOU

MATTHEW 5—THE HAPPY ATTITUDES

MATTHEW 6:9–13—THE LORD'S PRAYER

MATTHEW 6:25–34—DON'T WORRY

MATTHEW 7—ASK, SEEK, KNOCK

JOHN 14:1–3—PREPARING A PLACE

1 CORINTHIANS 13—GOD'S LOVE COLLECTION

PHILIPPIANS 4:8—THINK ON THESE THINGS

Genesis 1 and 2—The Seven Gifts of Creation

On each day of Creation God gave the world special gifts. Unpack them with your family to help them remember what He created during Creation week.

Bible connection:
Genesis 1:1–2:3. This is the beautiful story of God creating the world.

THINGS YOU NEED:

- Seven gift bags numbered one through seven. Any gift bag will do, but perhaps you can find designs that illustrate some of the days of Creation
- Add some of the following items to the relevant bags
  - Day one—a torch or candle
  - Day two—water in a bottle and a jar of bubbles. Blow a bubble to illustrate the firmament around the earth
  - Day three—grass, flowers, vegetables, fruit, etc.
  - Day four—sun, moon, and star shapes
  - Day five—toy birds and fish
  - Day six—toy animals and people (dolls or photos)
  - Day seven—Bible, model church, etc.

Worship activities:
1. Read the story of Creation from the Bible or your children's favorite Bible storybook.
2. Talk about God finding the world dark and empty and coming every day to give it special gifts.
3. Open the gift bags in order and talk about the different, important, and amazing gifts God gave the world. Are there any gifts we could have managed without? What are your favorite gifts? Why was it important for God to give the gifts in this order?
4. If you want to give your children a challenge, remove the numbers from the bags, move them around, and see if they can arrange them in the correct order. Or take some of the items out of the gift bags and see whether your children can arrange the objects in the correct order or return them to the correct gift bags.

Prayer:
- Choose one of the gift bags and thank God for a few of the wonderful things that He made on that day.

Other ideas:
- Send your children on a creation hunt to look for examples, pictures, or models of things that God made on each day. Then put the objects they find into the gift bags.
- Make a garland with seven triangular flags cut from scrapbooking paper or construction paper. Number each flag. Let your children draw or stick pictures onto the flags of the things God made each day.

Psalm 23—Walking With the Shepherd

Psalm 23 describes the ups and downs of the Christian life. Help your children to experience this familiar psalm by creating an interactive walk through the verses.

Bible connection:
Psalm 23

THINGS YOU NEED:
Set up everything in order before worship begins:
- Verse 1—toy sheep and shepherd, or pictures of a sheep and shepherd
- Verse 2—green blanket to lie on and glass of water to drink
- Verse 3—white yarn to make a path of righteousness to follow to the "dark valley" and the "feast"
- Verse 4—a short obstacle course, a blindfold to make it dark, and a stick
- Verse 5—delicious snack "feast" served on an attractive table
- Verse 6—craft materials to make a heavenly home

Worship activities:
1. Read Psalm 23 together. Then take your children on an interactive walk through the verses, reading each Bible verse as you arrive at the appropriate place.
2. Let your children lie on the green blanket (pasture), drink the still water, and be refreshed.
3. Show them the yarn path to follow—the path of righteousness.
4. When they arrive at the valley of the shadow of death, blindfold them and give them a rod, but also be there to guide and "comfort" them through the dark place.
5. Then lead them to a table where they can have a snack or feast.
6. Finally, let them make a heavenly home out of the craft materials.

Prayer:
- Say the twenty-third psalm together as a prayer.
- Sing a song based on the psalm instead of praying.

Other ideas:
- Make up actions to illustrate the psalm.
- Make a story roll for the psalm by cutting a strip of felt 6 inches (15 cm) wide and at least 24 inches (60 cm) long. Add a toy shepherd and some sheep; yarn grass for pastures; a mirror for still waters; yarn to make a path, or a toy compass; black felt cut like a dark valley, and a crook made from a chenille wire; a small dollhouse table with a meal on it or a paper plate with the picture of a meal on it; a picture of heaven or a piece of gold cardstock cut into the shape of a house.
- Let your children place the objects in order along the story roll to help them learn the psalm.

73

Psalm 139—God Knows You

Even though there are billions of people in the world, you are so special to God that He knows every detail of your life.

Bible connection:

"You created my inmost being; you knit me together.... I praise you because I am fearfully and wonderfully made" (Psalm 139:13, 14, NIV). God knows us so well because He made every detail of our bodies.

THINGS YOU NEED:

• A stack of index cards or slips of paper
• Pens

Worship activities:

1. Read the Bible verses and imagine God being right there as soon as you began to form as a baby. Think of how wonderfully you have been made and how reassuring it is that God knows all about you.
2. How well do you know each other?
3. Give each person a few cards and a pen. Invite them to write questions that will help you to become even more closely acquainted. Sample questions: What would you like to do if you were given a million dollars to help other people? What is your favorite fruit? What would be the best gift anyone could ever give you? Describe one of your happiest moments. If you could spend a day doing whatever you wanted, what would you choose to do? Where's your favorite place in the world? What would you like to be doing in ten years' time? Who's your favorite Bible character? Which time in history would you like to live in for a week?
4. Shuffle the cards and place them upside down on the table. Take turns picking a card and answering the question.
5. Make a list of everything you know about God.
6. Even though you have all learned more about each other by playing this game, God still knows more about each of you than you'll ever know about each other.

Prayer:

• Make your fingerprints using an ink pad and paper. See how they are all different. Try and guess which fingerprint belongs to which person. Thank God that He has made each of us unique and that He cares about the tiniest details of our lives, such as our fingerprints.

Other ideas:

• Look at a piece of your hair or skin under a microscope and see how wonderful it is. Or look for pictures on the Internet of skin, cells, and hair taken through a microscope.
• Read books and watch videos that highlight the wonder of human bodies and the development of babies before birth.

74

Matthew 5—The Happy Attitudes

Jesus described some unusual places to find happiness in His beatitudes.

Bible connection:

Matthew 5:1–12, the Beatitudes. Even when we think life is tough or sad, Jesus is working to bring us real happiness.

THINGS YOU NEED:

- Smiley face stickers (or draw smiley faces instead)
- Plain index cards or small sheets of paper, pens
- Preparation:
  - Write the beatitudes on index cards, with the first part of a verse (e.g., "Blessed are the peacemakers . . .") on one index card and the second half on another index card (e.g., ". . . for they will be called children of God."). Include the Bible reference on the second card. Place all the first parts of the verses in separate envelopes, and seal each envelope with a smiley face sticker, or draw a smiley face instead.
  - Set up an "out-of-place" treasure hunt by choosing a household object (1) to give to your children at the start of the hunt. In the place where object 1 usually lives, put an out-of-place object (2). In the place where object 2 usually lives, place object 3, and so on. Each time your children return an object to its proper place, they'll find the next object that needs returning. Replacing the out-of-place objects will lead them on a trail. The last object needs to be returned to the place where you have worship.
  - Place one of the prepared envelopes alongside each out-of-place object.

Worship activities:

1. Read the Bible passage. Explain that *blessed* can also mean "happy," and that Jesus helps us to be happy in difficult situations because we can trust Him to make everything work out well in the end.
2. Give the children object 1 and explain how the trail will work. Ask them to put everything back neatly and to collect the envelopes along the way.
3. When they have collected all the envelopes, open them and match the first half of each verse to the second half.
4. Ask, If you were to make a list of things that make people really happy, what would you include and why?

Prayer:

- Take each of the beatitudes and pray for a person described in the verse, such as someone who is merciful, persecuted, or sad. Pray that they will experience the happiness that Jesus promised in the rest of the verse.

Other ideas:

- Older children might like to rewrite the beatitudes in their own words.
- Make list of the unusual places and experiences where you and your family have discovered unexpected joy.

75

Matthew 6:9–13—The Lord's Prayer

Jesus gave us a simple and straightforward prayer to pray to God.

Bible connection:

Matthew 6:9–13, the Lord's Prayer. This prayer is a good pattern for our prayers. It starts with praise, and then continues with a desire to do God's will, a request for our basic needs, a time of confession and forgiveness, and a request for God's guidance and protection.

THINGS YOU NEED:

- Paper, pens, and coloring materials
- Prepare for worship by writing each phrase of the prayer on a separate sheet of paper

Worship activities:

1. Read or say the Lord's Prayer together.
2. Lay out the papers on which you have written the different sections of the prayer.
3. Let each person choose one or two phrases of the prayer to illustrate in any way they like. They can draw pictures, write thoughts, find objects, or create anything that illustrates the sections that they've chosen.
4. Give everyone 10 minutes to work.
5. Then arrange your sections in order, around your table, and look at what each person has drawn, found, written, or created.
6. Walk around the table as you say the prayer together.

Prayer:

- Write out each section of the Lord's Prayer, leaving a space below each phrase. Give one to each member of the family and invite them to write their own thoughts, praises, prayers, confessions, thanks, etc. under the relevant section of the prayer.
- Try singing the prayer to the traditional tune of "Auld Lang Syne" as it was sung by Sir Cliff Richard during the 2000 millennium celebrations.

Other ideas:

- Make a story roll to illustrate the Lord's Prayer. See the story roll instructions in the section "Worships Exploring Bible Stories."
- Search the Internet for interesting examples of the Lord's Prayer—videos, songs, posters, etc.
- Invite older children to make an illustrated PowerPoint presentation of the prayer.

— 76 —

Matthew 6:25–34—Don't Worry

God doesn't want us to be worried about our basic needs for food and clothes. He wants us to trust Him to provide everything we need, like a loving and caring Father.

Bible connection:

Matthew 6:25–34. Jesus told His followers not to worry about their clothes and their food because our Father knows everything we need and is continually providing for us.

THINGS YOU NEED:

- Chenille wires
- Cardstock, colored paper, scissors, pens, adhesive tape, etc.
- Small pot
- Permanent marker
- Coins and small stones
- Sturdy plant canes or popsicle sticks

Worship activities:

1. Read the Bible verses together. Jesus is tenderly telling His followers not to worry about the everyday details of their lives.
2. What are each of your concerns and worries? Cut spiky or wobbly shapes from colored cardstock and write a worry or concern on each shape. Tape each worry or concern to the end of a chenille wire.
3. Place all the "worry wires" in a small pot so that they can wobble. People are like the chenille wires, and they can feel very wobbly when they're holding on to worries and concerns by themselves.
4. Some of your worries might be very heavy. Tape some coins or small stones to the cardstock of your biggest worries to make the wires bend.
5. Write "God" on the popsicle sticks or sturdy plant stems. Tape each chenille wire firmly to a stick or cane so that the "God" sticks can support the chenille wires and take the weight of the "worries."
6. Use the marker pen to write "Don't worry, trust God!" on the pot.

Prayer:

- Let each person choose one of their concerns and worries—they can hold their worry if they wish. Gather around each person in turn. Place your hands on their shoulders and pray a sentence or two, asking God to untangle their concerns and fill them with peace.

Another idea:

- Cut flower (lilies of the field) or bird (sparrow) shapes out of colored paper. Write some of your worries and needs on these shapes. Cut out a large wing from paper or cardstock, and place your worries under God's wings, or cut large hand shapes and place your worries into God's hands.

Matthew 7—Ask, Seek, Knock

Jesus told us to ask God for help, to look for the many ways He might be answering our prayers, and to go right up and knock on His door whenever we need Him.

Bible connection:

"Ask and it will be given to you; seek and you will find; knock and the door will be opened to you" (Matthew 7:7, NIV). When we pray, we also need to keep our eyes open for God's answers and to knock on doors until God opens the right ones for us.

THINGS YOU NEED:

- Six index cards or pieces of paper decorated as follows: a picture of a mouth and the word "ask"; a picture of a gift and the words "and it will be given to you"; a picture of eyes looking and the word "seek"; a picture of something being discovered and the words "and you will find"; a picture of a door knocker and the word "knock"; a picture of an open door and the words "and the door will be opened to you." Don't number any of the cards.
- Pens and adhesive
- Assorted craft supplies for the prayer

Worship activities:

1. Before worship hide the cards you have made in different places. Your children will need to "ask" you to give them some cards; "seek" some cards you have hidden around the room, and "knock" on some cupboard, closet, or room doors to find other cards.
2. Read Matthew 7:7 together. Tell your children that they need to find six cards and that the Bible verse has given them all the clues they need. If they're not sure what that means, encourage them to look at the verse again until they realize that they need to ask, seek, and knock to find the cards.
3. Give the children what they ask for as soon as they ask, and open the doors as soon as they knock.
4. When they have found all the cards, see if they can put them in the right order to make the verse. Talk about God being a good Father and how much He wants to give us the best gifts when we ask Him.

Prayer:

- Make a key fob, poster, or small card, etc. with the acronym ASK on it. This will remind you to Ask God, to Seek God, and to Knock on doors looking for God when you are praying. Pray an ASK prayer: Example: Please God we are Asking for your help with ... Help us to Seek You until we find out what You want to do about the problem, and to keep Knocking on Your door until You open the best one for us. Thank you. In Jesus' Name, Amen.

Another idea:

- Make a door-hanger sign with the Bible verse written on it. This will remind your children to keep praying about their concerns and to trust that God is hearing them and working on the best solution to their problems.

78

John 14:1–3—Preparing a Place

Jesus has spent hundreds of years making heaven for us! It will be wonderful beyond our wildest dreams! But we can still imagine, share our ideas, and wonder what it will be like.

Bible connection:

John 14:1–3. Jesus knew He would soon leave His disciples, so He gave them a lovely message of peace and hope and the promise of heaven.

THINGS YOU NEED:

- Old shoeboxes or similar room-shaped boxes
- Scraps of attractive paper and craft supplies
- Small boxes, bits of junk and packaging
- Marker pens, scissors, etc.
- Glitter glue and assorted gold, silver, and gemstone-type craft supplies
- Adhesive and double-sided adhesive tape

Worship activities:

1. Read the Bible verse. Imagine Jesus preparing heaven for us, just because He loves us so much and He wants us to live with Him forever.
2. In some versions of the Bible, Jesus is preparing rooms for us in heaven. What do you think your room will be like? Do you think everyone's room will be the same, or will Jesus make each of our rooms unique, full of the things we like and enjoy?
3. Talk about what Jesus might put in a room that He was making for each one of you. What colors would He put on the walls and the floor? What kind of bed might there be? Would your room include special tools for developing your hobbies and interests? Will there be a Bible in your room? Will you still need lights? Or a wardrobe? Or a mirror? What do you think?
4. After sharing your ideas for a while, give each person a box in which to make their heavenly homes. Parents can help younger children to make their models. They can be as simple or elaborate as you wish.
5. Show each other your rooms and tell what else you would like to put into your room.
6. This project may last for several worships. If so, talk about your hopes and dreams for heaven and know it will be even better than anything you can ever imagine!

Prayer:

- Write John 14:1–3 on the side of each model. Recite the verses together.
- Thank God for the special places He is preparing for you in heaven.

Other ideas:

- Build your heavenly homes out of construction toys, such as Legos. Or use dollhouse furniture and other toys to help you design your rooms.
- Older children might enjoy make scale drawings, like architectural designs, instead of making models, or making a mood board of colors, furniture, fabrics, and accessories, etc., as if they were an interior designer.

1 Corinthians 13—God's Love Collection

Love is not a feeling—it is a verb. Love only becomes real when we put it into practice and when it makes a positive difference to our relationships.

Bible connection:
I Corinthians 13

THINGS YOU NEED:

A collection of a variety of different things that illustrate love in some way. You will only be able to find these once you have talked about the Bible verses.

Worship activities:
1. Read I Corinthians 13.
2. Make a list of all the definitions and descriptions of love contained in the verses. Then discuss how you could illustrate them with some of the things you already have in your home.
3. For example: Love protects—egg box, key, bubble wrap; love is patient—puzzle, construction kit; love is kind—hand lotion, something soft; love is forgiving—stain remover, chalkboard and eraser, soap.
4. Or talk about the times when God, or a human being, has shown you love in some of these different ways.
5. Or think of at least three Bible characters who showed the various qualities of love, such as patience (Abraham, Moses), kindness (Rebekah, Dorcas, Abigail), protection (Noah, Rahab, David).
6. Plan a specific and practical way your family could show love to someone else by being patient, kind, forgiving, uplifting, hopeful, protective, etc.

Prayer:
• Invite each person to choose an item that represents the aspect of God's love that they most want to experience, most want to develop in their lives, or most want to thank Him for today. Thank God for His love. Ask Him to help you show more of His love to those around you.

Other ideas:
• If you feel more adventurous, create a canvas of some of the "specimens" of God's love described in this verse. Print little labels of the definitions of love using your computer and cut them out. Arrange tiny heart-shaped objects or pictures that illustrate the definitions in rows. Fasten them securely. Use sticky foam tabs to stick the labels below the items to create a traditional specimen-box appearance.
• Or make a shadow box filled with items that illustrate God's love, using the things you found during worship. A shadow box is like a deep frame with several shelves or spaces for displaying objects, rather than pictures.
• Start a collection of stories from your family, the Bible, the Internet, the newspaper, etc. that illustrate the different aspects of I Corinthians 13 love.

(80)

Philippians 4:8—Think on These Things

It's very important for our children, and us, to keep our minds healthy and to focus on positive thoughts and ideas.

Bible connection:

"Finally, brothers and sisters, whatever is true, whatever is noble, whatever is right, whatever is pure, whatever is lovely, whatever is admirable—if anything is excellent or praiseworthy—think about such things" (Philippians 4:8, NIV).

THINGS YOU NEED:

- Paper, scissors, glue, and pens
- Small gold-colored gift boxes or bags
- Alphabet beads, blocks etc.—three W letters per person or small, blank cards

Worship activities:

1. Read the Bible verse, then write each of the thought categories listed in the Bible verse at the top of a different sheet of paper: True, Noble, Right, Pure, etc.
2. Then take turns sharing a positive thought and discussing which category it belongs to. Write it under the appropriate heading.
3. Then discuss what to do with thoughts that don't fit into one of those headings, thoughts that are lies, wrong, impure, discouraging, etc.
4. Usually our negative thoughts tell us that we're not good enough, people don't like us, or we always do things wrong, etc. We need to catch those unhelpful thoughts quickly and put them in the garbage!
5. Give each person a gift box or bag and slips of neatly cut paper to fit inside. Ask them to think of three thoughts that are true, noble, right, pure, lovely, etc. and to write them on separate slips of paper to keep in their gold box or bag.
6. Also ask them to write one positive thought to give to each of the other members in the family, for them to keep in their gift boxes.
7. Encourage everyone to add fresh thoughts to their positive thought boxes.

Prayer:

- Give each person the materials to make a small item that has the letters WWW on it. WWW stands for "What went well?" Encourage them to think about what went well each day, just before they go to sleep, and to thank God for what went well.
- Pray a WWW prayer together, with each person thanking God for something that went well today.

Other ideas:

- Give your children a cardstock party crown to decorate. Ask them to write the Bible verse on the crown, to remind them to think positive and lovely thoughts. Decorate the crown with craft supplies.
- Invite your creative children to make a lovely poster of this Bible verse to hang in your home.

SECTION 9

Character-Building Worships

DEVELOPING YOUR CHILDREN'S CHARACTER STRENGTHS

WISDOM

PEACE

GRATITUDE

LOOKING FOR THE GOOD

PERSEVERANCE

GENEROSITY

OBEDIENCE

PATIENCE

RESOURCEFULNESS

LOVE

Developing Your Children's Character Strengths

As Christians, our goal is to become more like Jesus and to help our children become more like Him too. This means working with Him to develop our character strengths. Character strengths describe what we're capable of doing when we're performing at our best. We can choose to nurture and develop various strengths by practicing them whenever we can.

Character strengths don't just help us to become more like Jesus, they also add extra quality to our everyday lives. The more character strengths we use, the happier we are and the more likely we are to be emotionally healthy, joyful, resilient, and able to cope with life's crises.

Building character strengths
- Make a list of character strengths that are important to your family. You will find some ideas in the activity list below.
- Draw a house with brick walls and write each of the character strengths from your list on a different brick. Make this together with your children. Above the house write "What character strengths are you building today?" Put it in a place where you'll see it every day.
- Have regular conversations during which you ask your children which character strengths they have used in the past day or week, and what happened when they used them. Look for what went well and give lots of positive encouragement.
- Plan projects and events that will help your children to practice specific character strengths. Make these fun and enjoyable so that your children enjoy developing their characters.
- Have character-strength days or weeks, during which you all choose to work on specific character strengths. Talk about your experiences together.
- Ask God to help you all develop your character strengths.

Character-strengthening activities*
Character-strength surveys for adults and children are available online at http://www.authentichappiness.sas.upenn.edu.

Listed below are some of the universally valued character strengths, along with some ideas to help you develop these character strengths together.

Appreciating beauty enriches your children's lives and helps them to notice the wonderful things around them.
- Look at a sunset, a shell, a flower, or a picture in a book and ask your children what they think is the most beautiful part of it.
- Tell each other the most beautiful thing you saw today.
- Visit art galleries or go for walks in nature, and help your children pause and notice beautiful things.
- Send them on a treasure hunt to find three beautiful things in the house, the garden, in a park, etc.

---

* These character strength ideas were previously published in *LIFE.info* magazine: "Building your child's character" by Karen Holford. Used with permission.

Caution helps your children to be safe and to avoid saying and doing things they'll regret later.

- Teach your children important safety skills and how to look out for dangers when they're climbing, flying kites, playing near water, etc.
- Help your children think about different ways of responding to a situation. Encourage them to consider the effects of what they might say and do to others, to themselves, and to the things around them.
- Use stories to help your children think about the positive and negative effects of each character's actions and what the characters could have done differently if they'd been more thoughtful.

Courage is facing up to difficult, challenging, or frightening situations instead of working out how to avoid them.

- If your children are fearful or shy, help them to think through the various things that make them feel afraid, to prepare well, and to find useful ways to manage their fears.
- Be there with plenty of reassurance and support when they're on the stage, at the dentist, facing an exam, etc.
- Help children to remember their brave times. Make a simple bravery award and write their brave moments on it, to encourage their courage in the future.

Creativity isn't just about being artsy-craftsy. Creativity is having an open mind about how things can be made and used, having a vision for an end product, and being determined to overcome the challenges of making it.

- Choose an everyday object, such as a rain boot, an empty jar, or a lone sock, and brainstorm at least ten crazy and practical ways it can be used.
- Let your children pick three fruit ingredients to invent a new kind of smoothie or try out different toppings on a pizza.
- Give your children a large cardboard box, some scissors, and a set of chunky felt pens and help them make it into a spaceship, a house, or whatever their imagination suggests.

Enthusiasm is doing things with energy and excitement rather than complaining.
- Be as enthusiastic as you can be—your enthusiasm is infectious!
- Create an enthusiastic ritual together—your own version of a high-five—and use it to inspire a bit of enthusiasm when your children are reluctant to get going.
- Say, "If we can all be ready and in the car in ten minutes, we can all have a special treat when we get there." This encourages children to help each other get ready quickly and adds a sense of excitement to getting out the door on time.

Fairness is treating all people equally, regardless of their differences.
- Teach your children how to share generously and equally with others and how to include new and lonely people in their playground games.
- Encourage them to have friends with different abilities and cultural backgrounds.
- Show respect and thoughtfulness to everyone you meet.

Forgiveness is being able to forgive those who hurt you and knowing how to let go of your hurt and resentment.
- Help your children to find symbolic acts to illustrate forgiveness, like washing dirt off a stone or writing letters and tearing them up.

- Teach your children that resentment fills them with sadness and pain, and that letting go of resentments gives them extra space to feel happy again.
- Help your children to do something kind for those who have hurt them, or those they have hurt.

Gratitude is being thankful for gifts and blessings and not taking things for granted.
- Say a traditional grace before meals.
- Find a diary with a small space for each day. At bedtime invite your children to think of three things they're thankful for and write them in the diary.
- Make attractive thank-you cards with your children. Encourage them to send cards for the smallest gift or kindness.

Honesty is telling the truth, even when it's hard, and being genuine and authentic.
- Respond warmly and lovingly to your children's honesty about the mistakes they have made; don't punish them for being truthful.
- Teach them how to tell the truth with love, sandwiching a sentence of thoughtful and considerate honesty between kind and encouraging words.
- Live honestly and transparently yourselves, without cheating or deceiving.

Hopefulness is about believing that the best things happen when you work to achieve your goals.
- Help your children set goals for their day, week, month, and year, depending on their age. Show them how to break goals into smaller steps so they can measure their progress.
- Make a paper star or candle shape and fill it with inspiring messages that nurture your children's hope.

Humor is best when people laugh together—and not at each other's expense. Enjoy having fun with your child.
- Tell each other the funniest thing you saw, heard, or did during the day.
- Go to a zoo and watch the funny antics of the animals.
- Look for the funny side of your life together.
- Do unusual and funny things. Wear your clothes backward for an hour, arrange slices of fruit to make a funny face, and hide funny things in their bed or lunchbox.

Kindness is being thoughtful about what another person needs and then putting that person's needs before your own.
- Involve your children in your own acts of kindness—bake a cake for someone, fill a basket with goodies for a sick friend, pack a shoebox of essentials for an overseas child. Let them have fun choosing the gifts and experiencing the joy of giving.
- Make a kindness kit for your children's school bags. Include a packet of fun tissues, bandages with smiley faces, a tasty cereal bar, a tiny fun toy, etc. Encourage them to share these with children who are hurt, sad, or hungry.
- Encourage your children to notice when others are tired, ill, or sad and to find ways to be kind to their family, teachers, and friends.

Self-control is being able to wait for what we want and to limit what we take and eat, etc.
- Offer your children the choice of a small treat now or a bigger treat later. Help them work through the benefits of waiting.

- Encourage children to take the smallest piece and to offer treats to others first before taking for themselves.
- Don't always buy what children want right away. Encourage them to wait a month to check if it's still what they really want.

Sociability is being aware of other people's feelings, as well as your own, and meeting their needs for comfort, encouragement, appreciation, help, respect, etc.

- Sociability is being able to share in each other's feelings. Encourage your children to be sad with those who are sad and to be happy with those who are happy.
- When you read stories, talk about what the characters might be feeling and needing, and what your children could do to be thoughtful and kind to them.

Spirituality is about believing that life has value, meaning, and purpose. It includes helping your children to learn about your own faith, or discovering God together, and developing a positive relationship with Him.

- Read biographies of people who were motivated to do great things because of their faith in God.
- Pray with your children.
- Tell your children that they are a gift from God to the world, that He loves them, and that He has a special, exciting, and happy plan for their lives.

Teamwork is being able to cooperate with other people in happy and supportive ways.

- Look for simple projects where you have to work together for the best results, such as putting up a tent, making a birthday party, flying a kite, or sailing a boat.
- Model teamwork by working alongside your children on challenging projects such as tidying their bedroom.
- Give your children plenty of opportunities to take part in team sports, music bands, and group performances, etc., depending on their interests.

Wisdom helps your children to make good choices.

- Write out some wise sayings and proverbs on plain cards. Take turns choosing a card and explaining what it means.
- When you read Bible stories, talk about the wisest people in the story and what they did and said that was so wise. Think about the foolish people, too, and learn from their silly mistakes!

81

Wisdom

Explore the book of Proverbs and discover many kinds of wisdom that can guide your life today.

Bible connection:

Matthew 2:1–12. The wise men recognized the special star and followed it to Bethlehem, where they found Jesus. They were wise because they followed the right star, because they had courage to make a long journey in difficult conditions, and because they obeyed God's warning not to return to Herod.

THINGS YOU NEED:

- Sheets of white or yellow paper or cardstock
- Scrap paper
- Marker pens and pencils
- Scissors
- Star template

Worship activities:

1. Before worship, cut one or two stars per person from the white or yellow paper or cardstock.
2. Choose a chapter in the book of Proverbs (after chapter 10) and read it together from a modern translation.
3. Let each person choose the verse that they like the best or that describes an area in which they need more wisdom.
4. Invite each person to rewrite their chosen proverb in modern-day language or in a way that applies best to their life. They can experiment by writing this on scrap paper first, until they find the best words.
5. Then write the final proverb paraphrases onto the stars. Make a mobile, garland, or display of the stars. Make a title banner that says "God's wisdom is the best guide for my life."
6. Talk about wisdom together: When have you made a wise choice? How did God or the Bible help you to make a wise choice? What is the wisest advice anyone ever gave to you?

Prayer:

- Read James 1:5 about asking God for wisdom.
- Take a plain paper star and pass it around the family circle. The person holding the star prays and then passes the star to the next person.
- Use this outline for your prayer: Praise God for His amazing wisdom, thank Him for sharing it with us through the Bible, ask God to forgive you for making unwise choices; and ask God to help you become wise.

Other ideas:

- Ask friends, family, and other church members to tell you which Bible verses help them to make wise choices.
- When you or your children don't know what to do, read the Proverbs until you find some wise and helpful advice.

Peace

When we live together in harmony, our relationships are happier and we are a powerful witness to God's peace in a world of chaos, pain, and conflict.

Bible connection:

"Blessed are the peacemakers, for they will be called children of God" (Matthew 5:9, NIV). Read the story of Jacob and Esau's family (Genesis 27, 28), or of Joseph and his brothers (Genesis 37 and 42–47), and think about what each person could have done differently to bring about peace in their family.

THINGS YOU NEED:

- Bible concordance
- White cardstock and white paper
- White feathers, tissue paper, and other collage items (optional)
- White thread
- Pencils, erasers, marker pens, scissors, and glue
- Dove pattern. Search the Internet for designs or draw your own

Worship activities:

1. Think about what helps you to live together peacefully in your family. Focus on the times when you manage your conflicts and disagreements well, and think about what helps you to do that.
2. Ask each person how they feel when others are arguing and how they feel when everyone is peaceful and happy.
3. Make some simple doves using white cardstock and paper.
4. On the body of each dove write some of your ideas for living together peacefully. Use a concordance and look through verses in Proverbs, Romans 12, 1 Corinthians 13, etc. to find out what the Bible says about living together lovingly and peacefully.
5. Decorate your doves with white collage materials.
6. Read what everyone has written on their doves. Ask each person what he or she would like to do to help make your family a more peaceful place.
7. Punch a hole in the top of each dove so that it will balance well when it is hung. Tie your peace doves from some branches arranged in a vase or from an old clothes hanger.

Prayer:

- Research a war-torn area of the world. Read the latest news about the situation, find the place on a map, and pray for peace.

Other ideas:

- Make a soothing and peaceful basket or box. Fill it with things that help you to feel peaceful, such as soothing worship music, a promise box filled with peaceful and encouraging Bible verses, a prayer for peace, a soft toy, a battery-operated flickering candle, or scented hand cream.
- Read biographies or watch documentaries of people who have been peacemakers in the world. What can you learn from them about peacemaking in your family and community?

83

Gratitude

What are you most thankful for? What are the tiny, everyday blessings that you take for granted? How can you encourage your family to be more thankful? Being thankful to God makes us feel happy and loved!

Bible connection:

"Always giving thanks to God the Father for everything, in the name of our Lord Jesus Christ" (Ephesians 5:20, NIV). How many of God's blessings have you thanked Him for, and how many have you forgotten to thank Him for?

THINGS YOU NEED:

- Small metal boxes with lids, plastic boxes, or matchboxes; keep them quite small
- Sticky labels, marker pens, glue, and collage materials to decorate the boxes

Worship activities:

1. Go on a gratitude treasure hunt around your home.
2. Give each person a small box and ask them to fill it with tiny items that remind them to thank God. It's surprising how many items you can fit in a small space!
3. Ideas: a grain of rice, a button (clothes), a small coin (money), a seed, a nut, a postage stamp, a small photo, a tiny toy brick, a stone, a shiny star, a raisin, a grain of salt, a pinch of herbs. Be as creative as you like!
4. Come back together and show what you found. Who has the most items in their box? Who found the most interesting or unexpected item?
5. Decorate the boxes, if you wish, with labels that say "Thank You, God, for every little thing!"

Prayer:

- Pray a thank-You circle prayer. The first person prays: "Thank You, God, for . . ." and names something that makes him or her feel thankful. The second person prays: "Thank You, God, for . . ." and then repeats the first person's thank you and adds another of his or her own. Continue doing this for a few rounds, but stop before it becomes too challenging for your children to remember them all.

Other ideas:

- Choose any room in your home. Go there together and look at the main objects in the room. Say, "Thank You, God, for this chair because it's so relaxing to sit in"; "Thank You, God, for this light that helps us to see at night"; "Thank You, God, for the photo of grandma and grandpa—we love them so much," etc.
- Set up a thank-You bowl or basket on your dinner table. Choose a night each week when you will eat together, and ask each person to put something in the bowl that represents what they want to thank God for that week.

84

Looking for the Good

Being able to see the good in challenging situations and in other people is an important character strength that brings hope and happiness.

Bible connection:

"Finally, brothers and sisters, whatever is true, whatever is noble, whatever is right, whatever is pure, whatever is lovely, whatever is admirable—if anything is excellent or praiseworthy—think about such things" (Philippians 4:8, NIV).

THINGS YOU NEED:

- A large box or bowl of dirt, sand, or small grains
- Spoons, sieves, forks, magnifying glasses
- Tiny beads, acrylic gems, small coins, tiny semiprecious stones, pieces of construction toys, and other "treasures" that will appeal to your children and won't be spoiled by the dirt
- Pieces of trash, such as polystyrene packaging or shredded paper
- Small bags or boxes in which to keep any found "treasures"
- Disposable gloves to keep hands clean
- Preparation: Stir tiny beads, acrylic gems, coins, and other treasures into the box or bowl of dirt, sand, or small grains. Do this outside, or cover the floor so the dirt doesn't make a mess. Make sure all the treasures are hidden. Prepare an individual bowl for each child.

Worship activities:

1. Read the Bible verse. Take turns telling the best thing you have noticed about each other in the past week.
2. Bring out the pans or bowls of dirt. On the surface they look plain and ugly.
3. Then tell them that the dirt is full of tiny treasures. They just need to dig and look, but they mustn't tip the dirt out of the bowls.
4. Allow them 5 to 10 minutes to dig and see how many treasures they can find. They can keep their treasures in their treasure bags.
5. Ask, "Can you think of situations that look too difficult to manage or people who are too hard to love? How are they like the pans of dirt?" They may look gloomy or unattractive on the outside, but tiny "gems" are always included—happy moments in the difficult times and beautiful characteristics in the most unlovely people. We just need God's help to find them.

Prayer:

- Think about some of the difficult situations or people your family is experiencing at the moment. Thank God for some of the gems hiding in the situation or for beautiful characteristics in a challenging personality.

Another idea:

- Find some puzzle pictures that have interesting things hidden in them when you look closely, such as the *Look-Alikes* and *Look-Alikes Jr.* books by Joan Steiner. Use them to illustrate the need to look closely for good things in people and situations.

85

Perseverance

Perseverance keeps us going when we're facing a challenge, when we're working on a long project, or when there's no one to help us or encourage us.

Bible connection:

"For this very reason, make every effort to add to your faith goodness; and to goodness, knowledge; and to knowledge, self-control; and to self-control, perseverance; and to perseverance, godliness" (2 Peter 1:5, 6, NIV). Perseverance gives us the strength to keep going, even when it's very hard.

THINGS YOU NEED:

- A completed jigsaw puzzle with 30 to 50 pieces for each child. Adjust the size of the jigsaw to your child's ability and patience.
- Use a construction toy model if a jigsaw wouldn't be appealing
- Cardstock, cut into large jigsaw-piece shapes, and pens

Worship activities:

1. Read the scripture reading and talk about perseverance. Tell each of your children about a time when you noticed them persevering at a difficult task, such as practicing the piano, reading a challenging book, making a difficult model, or working on their math homework.

2. Ask them why perseverance is important. Tell them about your own experiences of perseverance in a hobby, studies, or at work that were eventually rewarded.

3. Introduce the perseverance activity. You will sit in another room with the completed jigsaw puzzle or the pieces of a model and a copy of the instructions. Your children will make the model or puzzle in another room. If they are assembling a jigsaw, they must make it upside down.

4. Ask your children to come to you and collect one puzzle piece at a time and place it face down on their table. Then they can return to you and collect another piece, which will fit onto the pieces they already have.

5. You will give them the pieces in a random order, so they can't guess the position of the next piece. But every piece you give them must connect with a piece that they already have. They must repeat the process for each piece. As they work, try not to talk to them or encourage them, so they have to persevere on their own. It's not until they reach the very end that they can turn their puzzle over and see the finished picture.

6. Talk about perseverance together: how did it feel to do a repetitive, almost meaningless task? How did it feel to work alone and not be encouraged? What are they struggling to persevere with at the moment?

Prayer:

- Ask each person to write one challenge they want to persevere with on their large puzzle piece. Pray that each person will develop perseverance.

Another idea:

- Read the story of Thomas Edison. He persevered and made hundreds of light bulbs that didn't work before he invented one that did.

Generosity

Generosity is an important character trait that blends unselfishness, kindness, and a deep trust in God.

Bible connection:

"Freely you have received; freely give" (Matthew 10:8, NIV). God wants us to be generous with others, because He has been so generous with us.

THINGS YOU NEED:

- Large bags of individual ingredients for making a delicious trail mix—use your family's favorite ingredients—nuts, dried cherries, raisins, coconut, dried apricots, seeds, chocolate/carob/yogurt chips, etc.
- A large bowl per person for mixing their ingredients
- Wooden spoons
- A set of measuring cups and plastic cups
- Clean lidded jars or sealable plastic bags to make gift packs of trail mix
- White sticky labels and marker pens

Worship activities:

1. Make the trail mix gift packs and read the Bible passage after the activity.
2. First, give each person 1/4 cup of their favorite ingredient, giving everyone a different ingredient. Tell them the theme of the worship is generosity and that you are making trail mix to share. Then stand back and wait to see what they do.
3. When anyone decides to share an ingredient, give them a cupful of another ingredient in a plastic cup, so that it's easier to share. Soon they will work out that the more they share, the more they'll get.
4. Keep giving and sharing ingredients until everyone has a bowl of tasty trail mix.
5. Help them put their trail mix into jars or bags.
6. Write happy messages on the sticky labels, encouraging the recipients to share their trail mix with other people too.
7. Decide who will receive the gifts—teachers, friends, lonely people, etc.
8. Read the Bible verse. Everything we own has come from our generous Father in heaven, so we need to share generously with others.
9. Why is generosity an important character trait? Read 2 Corinthians 9:6–11.

Prayer:

- Pray with your hands palms up, and thank God for everything you have received so generously from Him. Pray with your palms down and ask God to help you be generous with the things He has given you.

Another idea:

- Think of someone you know who would appreciate a small gift or a card. Invite each child to contribute some of their money to the gift. Promise that whatever they give, you will give twice as much. Warmly appreciate their generosity. Go together to choose, buy, wrap, and deliver the small gift.

87

Obedience

Obedience nurtures several character strengths—respect, humility, love, and wisdom. The easier it is for us to obey our parents cheerfully and willingly, the easier it will be for us to obey God.

Bible connection:

"Children, obey your parents in the Lord, for this is right" (Ephesians 6:1, NIV). When children happily obey their parents, everyone feels safe and loved.

THINGS YOU NEED:

- The recipe, ingredients, and equipment to make a simple and healthful treat that your family enjoys, and that your children could manage to make with your instructions and supervision, such as flavored popcorn, a fruit smoothie, dried fruit and nut balls, pancakes, or waffles
- Cardstock, scissors, markers, and yarn

Worship activities:

1. Read the Bible verse. Thank your children for obeying you at a specific time during the past week. Tell them how much you appreciated their obedience and how happy and peaceful it helped you to feel, etc.
2. Ask them if they'd like to make the treat. Tell them that you'll give them clear instructions to follow. They will need to listen and obey carefully.
3. Give clear verbal instructions, one instruction at a time. Try not to repeat any instructions or to offer any advice or practical help.
4. See what happens. If it all goes smoothly and works perfectly, enjoy the results of their obedience. If something doesn't quite go according to plan, talk about what happened and why.
5. Discuss why obedience is so important. Ask your children to list the positive effects of obedience and the dangers of disobedience.
6. Why is it so important to obey God? What are the positive effects of obeying God, and what are the dangers of disobeying Him and His rules? Why do we sometimes disobey? What can help us to be more obedient?

Prayer:

- Write the word *God* in large, colorful letters on a sheet of cardstock. Punch holes along the bottom edge of the sheet. Write short prayers on shapes cut from scrap cardstock, asking God to help you obey Him more willingly and cheerfully, and overcome the proud and selfish thoughts that stop you from obeying Him quickly. Tie these to the God sheet to remind you that every act of obedience ties you closer to God.

Another idea:

- Switch roles for 15 minutes. Let your children become the parents while you pretend to be the children. Act out a time when your children might find it hard to obey, such as picking up their toys before bedtime. Pretend to be disobedient children for a short time, and see how your children respond in their role as "parents." This may help them to understand how their disobedience can be frustrating, tiring, and distressing to their parents.

Patience

Patience is an important character strength that helps us show love to others in several different ways. It's the first characteristic of love listed by Paul.

Bible connection:

"Love is patient" (1 Corinthians 13:4, NIV). What is patience? How does being patient with someone else show them our love, kindness, and respect?

THINGS YOU NEED:

- A printed or handwritten copy of 1 Corinthians 13:4-8 for each child. Carefully cut the phrases and verses apart between the rows and words, so that you have a pile of strips with words and phrases on them. Cut any verse numbers off the strips so there aren't any numerical clues, and cut larger sections of words for younger children
- Paper, pens, scissors, glue sticks

Worship activities:

1. At the beginning of worship give each child a set of 1 Corinthians 13:4-8 words, a sheet of paper, and a glue stick. Tell them that you need them to complete the Scripture reading as quickly as possible and that they must work as fast as they can to stick the words in the right order.
2. As soon as they start to work, pretend to be impatient and say, "Come on! Hurry up! Work faster!"
3. Let them work for 10 to 20 seconds under pressure, and then be patient and say, "It's OK. I'm sorry I was being impatient. There's no rush. Take your time. Enjoy the puzzle. Here's a Bible to help you put the words in the right order. Would you like me to help you?" etc.
4. When they have finished assembling the Bible passage, ask one of your children to read it aloud. Discuss why Paul listed patience before kindness and forgiveness when he was describing love.
5. Write on a sheet of paper: "When other people are patient with me I feel …" Write down everyone's answers, such as safe, peaceful, happy, loved, cared for, and special. On another sheet of paper write "When other people are impatient with me I feel …" Write down everyone's answers, such as afraid, stressed, rushed, stupid, uncared for, and misunderstood.
6. Write "Patience" on a sheet of paper. Write "Things I can say" at the top of one column and "Things I can do" at the top of the second column. List what you and your children can say and do to show patience to others.

Prayer:

- Thank God for His patience with you, ask Him to forgive you for your impatience with others, and ask Him to help you show other people His patient kindness and love.

Another idea:

- Think about a time or place in your family where you find it hard to be patient with each other, such as by the front door or at mealtimes. Make a fun sign to remind you all to be more patient with each other.

89

Resourcefulness

Being resourceful is about taking care of the world's resources, being good stewards of the things you own, and creatively using what's available to you. It helps you to be content, versatile, economical, generous, and thoughtful about how you buy and dispose of your things. Resourceful people look for possibilities, solutions, and opportunities rather than problems.

Bible connection:

"She wrapped him in cloths and placed him in a manger, because there was no guest room available for them" (Luke 2:7, NIV). Mary didn't have a bed for Jesus, so she put Him in an animal's feeding trough.

THINGS YOU NEED:

- A selection of six everyday objects such as an empty soda bottle, a rubber boot (wellington boot), a flowerpot, a plastic tote bag, an empty jelly (jam) jar; and a paper plate. Place them on a table, label and number them from one through six, and cover everything with a tablecloth or sheet.
- A six-sided game die

Worship activities:

1. Read Luke 2:7 and think about placing a new baby in a crib made from an animal's feeding trough!
2. Think of other unusual uses in the Bible: Jacob used a stone for a pillow, Samson used the jawbone of an ass as a weapon, bees used a dead lion as a beehive, Mary used her hair to wipe Jesus' feet, etc. God used a large fish to rescue Jonah, Jesus used water to make wine, and He transformed a small lunch to feed thousands of people. Can you think of other unusual uses?
3. Remove the cloth from your six objects and look at them. Discuss how they could also be used in creative and different ways.
4. Take turns rolling the game die. The person who rolls the die has to pick up the object with the same number as the die and think of one possible creative and unusual use for the object. For example, a boot can hold water, like a bucket; a jar can be used as a candle lantern; and a plastic tote bag can become a waterproof ground-seat. Ideas can't be repeated.
5. Or work together to think of ten creative ways to use each object.

Prayer:

- Thank God for all the wonderful resources He has given your family. Ask Him to help you to take care of them and to share them with others. Ask Him how He wants to use your skills and resources in ways you've never thought about before.

Another idea:

- Have a fun evening making small gifts for each other, using the things you already own in creative and unusual ways. Look for ideas on Web sites that specialize in recycled crafts, or find useful books in your library.

Love

Of all the character strengths, love is the greatest. The more we learn how to love, the richer and more beautiful the rest of our character strengths will become.

Bible connection:

"Now these three remain: faith, hope and love. But the greatest of these is love" (1 Corinthians 13:13, NIV). If love is the greatest, how can we love each other better?

THINGS YOU NEED:

- Paper, pens, colored cardstock, scissors, hole-punch, and yarn
- Coloring pencils or marker pens in red, green, blue, yellow, and purple

Worship activities:

1. Read the Bible verse about love.
2. Ask everyone to draw a large heart on their sheets of paper. Then ask them to write inside their heart six to ten things other people have done that made them feel especially loved.
3. Give them the coloring pens and ask them to circle the examples of love with different colored pens:
4. Draw a red circle around the times someone said or wrote something that helped you to feel loved.
5. Draw a green circle around the times when someone helped you in a practical way.
6. Draw a blue circle around the times when someone showed you love by hugging you or touching you (patting, tickling, etc.).
7. Draw a yellow circle around the times someone gave you a thoughtful gift.
8. Draw a purple circle around the times someone spent time with you, doing something you enjoyed.
9. Discuss what you have learned about how you like to be loved. How do the rest of the people in your family like to be loved? What can you do to help them feel especially loved?

Prayer:

- Thank God for loving you in all kinds of ways. Make a garland of cardstock hearts, each one describing a special experience of God's love.

Another idea:

- Make a list of special things you do that help each other to feel loved. Try to do something loving for each other at least once a day.

Worships for
Special Occasions

JESUS' BIRTH
A GIVING CALENDAR

PRESENT TIME!

JESUS' DEATH AND RESURRECTION
HOSANNA PRAISE FLAGS

CROSS SEARCH

CREATE A CROSS

HOPE ALIVE!

HARVEST AND THANKSGIVING
THANKSGIVING OR ADVENT SHARE

SPIRIT FRUITS

A GARLAND OF GRATITUDE

BIRTHDAYS
YOU'RE A GIFT!

91

A Giving Calendar

The story of Jesus' birth is about giving rather than receiving gifts. Giving to others is one of the best ways for you to feel happy too!

Bible connection:

Matthew 1:18–2:11; Luke 2:1–20. The familiar stories are full of people who gave up their dreams, time, possessions, space, and plans to take care of Jesus when He was homeless and vulnerable.

THINGS YOU NEED:

- An Advent calendar with empty pockets, boxes, or drawers (or paste 24 small, colorful, numbered envelopes onto a sheet of cardstock so that they can be opened and closed easily)
- A nativity set, old Christmas cards, or a storybook about Jesus' birth
- Brochures recruiting donations for charity projects

Worship activities:

1. Read the Bible story or use a children's Bible storybook.
2. Talk about the story of Jesus' birth. Pick up the various characters in the nativity set, or look at the pictures in the book. Discuss what each character might have given up, or given away, during the story: God, Jesus, Mary, Joseph, the innkeeper, the shepherds, the wise men, etc.
3. Look through the charity brochures and talk about what each of you can give up to help someone in need. Perhaps you could buy a goat or chickens for a family in Africa or give something to a local charity that helps children.
4. Create a sense of excitement about giving something that will make a huge difference to another family or child. Read Matthew 25:40 and talk about how everything we do to help others, we are also doing for Jesus. Whatever we give away to help others is a gift we are giving to Jesus.
5. Encourage your children to collect money each day, or week, in their Advent calendar. They can give some of their own money, ask other friends and relatives for contributions to their good cause, and do small tasks around the home.
6. When you've reached your target, celebrate together, and let your children play a part in giving your family's love gift to the people who need it.

Prayer:

- Pray for the people in need that your children know and ask God to help you understand the best way to help them.

Another idea:

- Instead of collecting money in the envelopes or calendar, write 24 simple ideas for helping others on individual index cards. Insert one card into each of the sections or envelopes. Do one activity each day. Ideas: finding three good unwanted toys to donate to charity, donating rice to a feeding project by playing the game at http://www.freerice.com, making cookies to give away, making a card to send to a person who is ill or housebound, making a goodie bag to give to a homeless person on the street, or doing a project to earn money toward a good cause.

92

Present Time!

This activity provides your family with an opportunity to give each other imaginary and wished-for gifts—the kinds of presents you would like to give each other … if only you could!

Bible connection:

"Every good and perfect gift is from above, coming down from the Father of the heavenly lights" (James 1:17, NIV). If we know how to give good gifts to each other, just think of the gifts that our loving father, God, would like to give us! Or maybe He has already given them to us, but we haven't discovered them, or opened them, yet?

THING YOU NEED:

- Blank greeting cards from a craft supplier or sheets of cardstock folded to make greeting cards
- Marker pens or crayons
- Pens and pencils
- Gift-wrapped box
- Sticky notes or labels

Worship activities:

1. Give each person a blank greeting card.
2. Ask them to draw a picture of a wrapped gift on the front of the card, including a gift tag with their name on it.
3. When everyone has finished, pass the cards around the circle. Invite each person to write inside each card a description of the gift they would like to give the card's owner if they could give them anything in the whole wide world.
4. When everyone has written in everyone else's cards, the cards are returned to their original owners so that they can read about the gifts everyone else wanted to give them.
5. Each person can thank everyone else for their virtual gifts and keep their card to remind them of everyone's generous thoughts.
6. Then discuss the best gifts that God has given your family and the gifts He might like to add to each of your cards.

Prayer:

- Place the gift-wrapped box on the table. Invite everyone to write or draw five things they want to thank God for on separate sticky labels or sticky notes. Stick the notes onto the gift box. Pass the gift box around your prayer circle and invite each person to read one of the labels as a thank-You prayer to God.

Another idea:

- Instead of writing in each other's cards, make each other virtual presents by folding, tearing, cutting, and drawing on sheets of blank paper. Then give your paper gifts to each other, telling each other what they are really meant to be, just in case it isn't obvious!

93

Hosanna Praise Flags

Celebrate your praises to God by creating praise flags together.

Bible connection:

Matthew 21:1–9. When Jesus rode into Jerusalem on a donkey, the people spontaneously praised Him and God. How would we praise Him today if He rode down a street near us?

THINGS YOU NEED:

- Green wooden plant sticks, wooden beads to make their ends safe
- Green paper
- Sticky tape, double-sided tape, or adhesive
- Scissors, marker pens, yarn

Worship activities:

1. Read the Bible passage and imagine what would happen if Jesus came to the area where you live. How would your town welcome Him? If you went out to see Him, how would you praise Him?
2. What are the various things you would each like to praise Jesus for?
3. Create "palm" flags using the green paper. Cut the flags into different leaf shapes and write praises on them.
4. Stick the leaf flags to the plant sticks with sticky tape.
5. Wrap some tape around the ends of the sticks so that they are not sharp, or glue large wooden beads onto the ends of the sticks.
6. Sing your favorite lively praise song and wave your flags together, or display them in a vase to remind you to praise God.
7. Ask, Why do we praise God? Does He need to be praised? Do we need to praise Him? Why is it so important for us to praise God?

Prayer:

- Make a praise garland. Cut green paper into 26 strips or leaves.
- Think of at least one thing to praise God for that begins with each letter of the alphabet. Write all the praises beginning with A on one strip or leaf and all those beginning with B on another leaf, and continue through the entire alphabet.
- Tape the strips to a long piece of yarn or string to make your praise garland.

Other ideas:

- Use colored papers to create multicolored flags. Cut out shapes that illustrate your praises, such as crowns, the world, stars, and crosses. Glue a paper collage on one side of your flag, and write your praises on the other side.
- If you have an experienced seamstress in your family, design and sew fabric praise banners for your family.

94

Cross Search

There are lots of cross shapes hidden in the world around us! We can find them in the patterns on windows, gates, paving stones, shelves, etc. Every cross we see can remind us that Jesus died to save us. We can also remember that He is no longer on the cross. He is alive and in heaven!

Bible connection:

"The message of the cross is foolishness to those who are perishing, but to us who are being saved it is the power of God" (1 Corinthians 1:18, NIV).

THINGS YOU NEED:

- Pencils
- Lined paper
- Scissors

Worship activities:

1. Read the Bible verse together and talk about why Jesus died on the cross for us.
2. Walk around your home, neighborhood, park, or church and look for crosses in interesting places—the shape of a door, the pattern in a window, a road sign, a fence, in furniture, tiles, fabric patterns, etc.
3. Write down all the different places where you found a cross shape.
4. See how many you can find in half an hour, or how long it takes to find 100!
5. Which was the most unusual cross you found? Which was the hardest to see?

Prayer:

- Draw the faint outline of a cross on several sheets of lined paper.
- Give one cross to each person.
- Write prayers inside the outline, thanking Jesus for dying on the cross to save us. Then read them aloud to each other.
- Cut out your crosses and pin them where they'll remind you how much Jesus loves you.

Other ideas:

- Take photographs of the crosses that you find and make a cross photo album or collage.
- Maybe the crosses you find will give you fresh ideas about Jesus and His love for you. A cross in a gate can remind you that Jesus is the way to heaven. A cross in a window can remind you that Jesus' death on the cross helps us to see our future more clearly.
- Search the Internet to find various crosses from around the world. Find out why they look so different.

95

Create a Cross

The empty cross of Jesus is a powerful Christian symbol that is rich with many different meanings. Try exploring some of these with your older children.

Bible connection:

"For the joy set before him he endured the cross, scorning its shame, and sat down at the right hand of the throne of God" (Hebrews 12:2, NIV).

THINGS YOU NEED:

- A wide range of different materials (you will know what you need to find when you know which cross each person is going to make)
- Scissors
- Glue
- Crayons
- Paints, etc.

Worship activities:

1. Invite each person to talk about the Bible verse and what the cross of Jesus means to him or her.
2. Perhaps the cross is comforting, loving, hopeful, painful, happy, or peaceful, etc.
3. Once everyone has talked about what Jesus' cross means to them, create a variety of crosses that represent your ideas. For example: a comforting cross could be cut from a scrap of soft fleece; a painful cross could be made from two large nails or from twisted wire; a new-life cross could be made out of budding twigs; a hopeful cross could be colored like a rainbow; and a loving cross could be covered in hearts. Parents may need to help younger children create their crosses.
4. When everyone has finished making their crosses, invite them to show the crosses they have made and to say what it means for them.
5. Display your crosses in a group, or try carrying them with you for a day.

Prayer:

- Make a paper-patchwork prayer cross. Cut squares of colored paper. Write your prayers of confession on the pieces of colored paper, and glue them, writing side down, onto a cardstock cross. Keep adding prayers and paper until the cross is covered. Cover everything with clear adhesive film to keep the prayers safe and private.
- Draw around your hands on sheets of paper. Cut out the hands and write prayers of confession on them. Attach your prayers to a small wooden cross or to a tree, using a hammer and nails.

Another idea:

- Work as a group instead of making separate crosses. Cut a cardstock or wooden cross and cover it with ideas, Bible verses, pictures, and objects that express what Jesus' death and resurrection mean to each of you.

Hope Alive!

This activity explores the story of Jesus' resurrection.

Bible connection:

Matthew 28:1–10. Even when things look hopeless to us, God can still do miracles. Jesus was dead and the disciples felt hopeless, but God brought Him back to life. Seeds may look dead, but they still contain life that can be "resurrected" with sunlight and water into something green and tasty.

THINGS YOU NEED:

- A rectangular plastic food tray
- Paper towels and water
- Cress or alfalfa seeds
- Pencil; scissors; tan, green, and brown paper

Worship activities:

1. After reading Matthew 28:1–10, think about the words that describe what the Resurrection means to you as a family. Choose one or two shorter words, such as hope, love, life, or joy.
2. Fold several sheets of paper towels to neatly line your food tray.
3. Draw the outline letters of your chosen word onto the paper towels, so that seeds can be "planted" inside the shapes of the letters. If these letters are hard to draw, use a large computer font to help you, and resize the word so that it fits within the edges of the food tray.
4. Use water to dampen the paper towels and then sprinkle cress or alfalfa seeds within the letter outlines.
5. Place the seeds in a warm, bright place and keep them damp so that they can sprout and grow to spell the word you have chosen.
6. The seeds that looked dead and lifeless will be resurrected to new life!
7. Cut the cress when it has grown and serve it in delicious sandwiches. You could even cut the sandwiches to spell the letters of your word!

Prayer:

- Invite each person to write one of their hopes on a piece of tan paper cut to look like a seed. Stick all of your hope seeds onto a sheet of brown paper and label it "The soil of faith." Cut a green paper shape of a simple watering can and write on it "Water regularly with prayer." Place this poster where it will remind you to pray for your hopes. Add paper flowers to the poster when a hope becomes a reality and your prayers are answered.

Other ideas:

- Work together to plant purple crocuses or other seasonal flowers in your front yard, to spell a word such as hope or a phrase such as Jesus is alive!
- Time your planting so that the words are visible or flowering for Easter.
- Plant bulbs to give away, and make plant tags or labels with brightly colored signs and Bible verses about hope and new life.

97

Thanksgiving or Advent Share

This activity encourages you and your family to share your blessings and to help others.

Bible connection:

2 Corinthians 9:6, 7. Whenever we give something away, God finds a way to give even more back to us. Whatever we give away, we are giving to God. How can we be more cheerful about our giving?

THINGS YOU NEED:

- Some strong cardboard boxes
- A home with too many things in it
- A worthy cause or Goodwill store that will accept your donated items. There may be some special things they need, or some things they don't want at all, so it's worth checking first.

Worship activities:

1. Read the Bible verses and talk about the importance of sharing what we have with others. When we have less clutter in our rooms and homes, it's also easier to keep them tidy, clean, and stress-free.
2. Set a target of collecting at least one good-quality item each day that can be given away to a charity or other worthy cause. Decide how many days you would like to collect things and divide them between the people in your family. For example: if you are collecting through the 24 days of Advent, and there are four of you in the family, you could donate six items each.
3. If you are doing this as a harvest or thanksgiving project, see how many unneeded things your family can harvest from your home in a week!
4. Talk about how it feels when we give things away. What makes it easy to give things away to others, and what makes it hard? Why do we keep buying more things? What would happen if we decided to give one or two things away every time we bought something new?

Prayer:

- Pray for the people who need the things you are giving away.

Other ideas:

- Help the younger members of the family to decorate the box in which you will collect all your unwanted items.
- Choose to go without a specific food item each day, and donate a nonperishable package of this food to your collection box. Take turns choosing which food your family will donate. Give the box to a needy family or homeless persons' charity. Make sure the box contains some treats, as well as plenty of nutritious and tasty food.

Spirit Fruits

This activity encourages your family to think about the fruits that the Holy Spirit wants to grow in your lives.

Bible connection:

Galatians 5:22, 23. Often our lives are filled with to-do lists, and we're busy thinking how we'll get everything done. But God is more interested in our "to-be" list and how we'll let His Spirit grow in our lives. He wants us to grow the good fruits that build healthy families and relationships.

THINGS YOU NEED:

- At least nine different kinds of fresh and dried fruit—more if possible
- A large basket or serving dish
- Plain white cards
- Pens

Worship activities:

1. Arrange the fruits in the basket or on the dish.
2. Write one of the fruits of the Spirit on each of the white cards: love, joy, peace, patience, kindness, goodness, faithfulness, gentleness, and self-control.
3. Read the verses in Galatians 5:22, 23.
4. Look at the fruits you have found and see whether you can match each of the fruits to one of the fruits of the Spirit written on a white card. For example: if you think that a peach reminds you most of love, then place the "love" card next to the peach. An apple might represent goodness; lemon—self-control; pomegranate—patience; strawberry—joy; banana—peace, etc. You will need to discuss the different characteristics of the Holy Spirit and how each fruit might illustrate that quality.
5. Ask, "How much of each fruit is growing in your life right now? Which fruits do you think the Holy Spirit *most* wants to grow in your life? How do these fruits help us to share God's love with each other?"

Prayer:

- Invite everyone to choose a fruit of the Spirit that they would like to grow more in their lives.
- Pray for the Holy Spirit to work in your lives and help your fruit to grow.

Other ideas:

- After you have matched the fruits to their spiritual characteristics, use them to make a smoothie or a fruit salad that you can enjoy together.
- Cut fruit shapes from colored paper. Write on each fruit the matching fruit of the Spirit that your family chose during your worship time. Laminate the fruits and cut them out again. Put a fruit by someone's dinner place when you've noticed that person showing one of the fruits of the Spirit. This will encourage them to grow more fruit.

A Garland of Gratitude

Create a gratitude garland to remember the wonderful blessings and events that your family has experienced during the past year.

Bible connection:

"Praise the LORD, my soul, and forget not all his benefits" (Psalm 103:2, NIV).

David reminds us to keep on remembering all the good things that God does for us. The memories of all of His blessings help to keep our faith in Him strong and alive. What are the good things that God has done for you this year?

THINGS YOU NEED:

- A base for your garland, such as a length of thick, brightly-colored yarn, tinsel, ribbon, or rope.
- Scraps of ribbon, strips of fabric, curling ribbon, yarn, twine, etc.
- Scissors, adhesive, and marker pens
- Luggage tags or old greeting cards and a hole punch
- Spare photos, small souvenirs, little objects, etc.

Worship activities:

1. Read the Bible verse. Then talk together about the past year and make a list of the blessings that your family has experienced and received during the past twelve months. Use your calendars, diaries, and photographs to help you remember some of the wonderful things that happened.
2. Think of small symbols, pictures, mementos, or objects that represent each of the good things or blessings that you've listed, and then hunt for them around your home.
3. Draw or stick pictures onto luggage tags. Cut pictures from greeting cards and punch holes in them.
4. Use recycled packaging ribbon, string, or fabric scraps to tie your objects to your garland base. Make a time line by attaching them in the order in which they happened.
5. Hang your gratitude garland in a special place where it will remind you of God's blessings.

Prayer:

- Take turns praying thank-You prayers for the various blessings you have tied onto your garland.

Other ideas:

- Create a simple paper chain. Write each blessing on a separate paper strip before constructing the chain.
- Make a garland of triangular-shaped flags or pennants. Draw or write your blessings on the triangles, or cut pictures from magazines to paste onto the flags. Write a short prayer of thanks on each flag, using the back of each triangle if you need more space.

100

You're a Gift!

A birthday worship

Bible connection:

"You created my inmost being; you knit me together in my mother's womb. I praise you because I am fearfully and wonderfully made" (Psalm 139:13, 14, NIV). Each person is a masterpiece, an artistic and amazing creation that God has gifted to the world.

THINGS YOU NEED:

- A large box, such as an appliance box
- A flashlight
- A pillow
- A large roll of gift wrap (optional)
- Sticky tape, paper, sticky notes, marker pens, etc.
- A gift they'll enjoy that will nurture their spiritual development

Worship activities:

1. Before a child's birthday, ask everyone else in the family to write: I'm so glad God gave you to our family because ..., and then write one reason for every year of their age. It doesn't matter if some of you write the same reasons. Keep these papers safe. Keep the spiritual gift hidden.
2. Then, before family worship, gift wrap the birthday child in a large box. Make sure he or she doesn't have to stay in the box for more than a few moments, in case he becomes afraid, bored, or uncomfortable. Give him a flashlight and a pillow, just in case.
3. Make the box look attractive in a quick and simple way, and leave the top open so that the birthday child can pop up quickly and "surprise" everyone.
4. Stick the "I'm so glad ..." messages on the outside of the box.
5. Call everyone to worship and tell them that the birthday child has missed opening the best gift. Sing "Happy Birthday" and then let the child pop up out of the box to be cheered and celebrated. *He or she* is the best gift because God made him and gave him as a special gift to your family. No other family in the world has this special and unique gift!
6. Let the child read what everyone wrote and stuck on the box.
7. Finally give him or her the spiritually nurturing gift.

Prayer:

- Write a prayer of blessing for your child on a birthday crown and place it on his head, or lay your hand on his head as you bless him. If you're not sure what to say, use the Aaronic blessing in Numbers 6:22–27.

Other ideas:

- Write a letter of thanks to God for your children each year. Give them the letters to read, and then keep them in an album with their birthday photo.
- If you have older children who would find the box idea childish, ask each person to write their "I'm glad ..." messages (as above) and include them with their cards or birthday gifts.